Window Box Gardening – A Practical Introduction

How to Grow Flowers of All Seasons on Your House or Apartment's Windowsills

By Tiffany Grant

Cover image credit: Valerie Everett, Spencer Means

About the Author

Tiffany Grant grew up in a country village in England, becoming familiar with many aspects of pastoral life at an early age. Her mother's love of window planters, placed within the kitchen and bedroom of the family home, left a lasting impression in complement to the flowery scenes and rolling fields. After university, Tiffany like many headed to the city to embark on her career. It was here, in a small apartment, that she found occasion to emulate her mother's hobby anew. Inspired to aid others in similar circumstances, Tiffany has transplanted anew the customs and guidance of window gardening into this primer.

Table of Contents

Preface

This book was written with the express aim of helping those who are resident in a small home or apartment without any conventional back yard or garden space to cultivate plants upon. Designed as an embracing beginner's guide, this book intends to imbue the aspiring grower with practical ideas, techniques and tips in tending a small crop of flowers.

Mindful of the seasonal changes which underpin the life cycle of many flowers, I have endeavoured to include examples of hardy yet beautiful plants which can thrive beneath the hand of a careful beginner during most of the year. Tending to these amid changing weather is a true task, with the inevitable mistakes and follies a test of persistence and good will in making this windowsill mounted containers burst forth with natural beauty.

Encouragement is given for growers to venture out and gather flowers from meadows and woods. While such an expedition is often out of reach for inhabitants of cities, it goes without saying that the specimens mentioned here are available in garden centers. While the absolute beginner can purchase pre-grown plants, the experienced gardener may opt to grow their plants from seed.

However you decide to embark on introducing some greenery to the grey and sterile surroundings of the modern city, be mindful of the calm and tranquillity which is so agreeable to the task. There is a meditative edge to inspecting, watering and tending to your little window garden – it is an opportunity to bond with the greenery, put aside the endless tide of information and stress, and (in a small way) return to the Earth which many of our ancestors spent lifetimes tending to.

Whatever your motives for starting a window garden; whether it's as a break for originality in a world where so many home dwellers are obsessively happy with electronic gadgets or TV; as a means of impressing and catching the eyes of passers-by; or simply as a relaxing nourishment for a soul stymied by the busy modern life, engage in the task with optimism and grace of a fresh shoot lapping up the sunshine.

Introduction

As my little book has been written chiefly for city dwellers, the plainness of language aimed at requires no apology from me; but in speaking of flowers, one can hardly help rising to a somewhat higher and more aesthetic or even poetic level. Gazing on their exquisite beauties, purer thoughts arise as we contemplate them in the quiet fields, lanes and woods, and wonder if we might have them dwell with us at home.

Beautiful flowers spread out in boundless fields are a pure enjoyment, and their localities are as varied as their hues. The corn-cockle and the poppy delight to revel in the sun: but the fern loves the solitude of the grove, in the twilight of the forest; the moss is its sweet companion.

Let us wander back to the days when we were young; when we played in parks and country among poppies, bluebells and daffodils. Who can behold them without delight? By what mind are they counted as a mere baubles - blooming and fading, for no end?

In addressing you the reader I would first ask – do you have a genuine love for flowers?

If you have a simple passion, then constructing a window garden will help you increase your enjoyment from such love. Should it happen that your love of flowers has been extinguished by a thousand drawbacks, I will do my best to rekindle the old flame. Perhaps it will burn brighter than ever.

On the other hand, if you have no love for flowers, no love for those innocent companions, and merely want something to do, then in all earnestness I encourage you to enter this beautiful department of nature, not merely as spectators, but as possessors and keepers of your own little grove. Who knows, in time you might feel a healthy compulsion as the germinal sprout of your own compassion for home gardening.

There's inspiration aplenty out there; many European cities are known for their festoons of beautiful flowers creeping up along the quaint balconies. They creep round the doors and curious windows; a pleasant splash of natural colour around the relative sterility of their brick, mortar and concrete surrounds.

The atmosphere of our fumy habitations forbids the existence of such enjoyments; but reasonable hope may be held out for the embellishment of windows of all dwellings, however situated, to be decorated with some form of vegetation. In crowded cities where residents may nearly shake hands with one another across the narrow street that divides their habitations, where the genial rays of the sun never penetrate, and where the impurities of the air offend the dullest sense, a few plants in the windows help to neutralize these facts; and to begin we have only to search for the natural elements which furnish us with something beautiful for our windows.

In advocating the culture of window-plants as a source from which no little enjoyment can be received, I am fully aware that all those who live in large towns are at many disadvantages. Strict landlords and apartment or housing complex rules, and even prohibiting citywide laws, can head off your ambition for a full-fledged window garden.

Should you clear these hurdles, instruction is still very much needed, as attempts to enter with any spirit on this innocent and instructive recreation are likely to fail. To many the greatest obstacle is knowledge in how to grow window plants, and the want of convenient windows for their cultivation. If these obstacles could not be overcome, I might give up the task of leading you forward to the paradise that is growing flora. Further along the line, herbs such as rosemary or mint offer ample opportunity to expand and benefit in a culinary fashion from your window garden.

Thousands of floral varieties can, with a little effort and skill, grow and thrive with bountiful gifts in the most unlikely localities; under the most adverse circumstances it gives me the greatest assurance to place before you a practical guide for acquiring a cultural knowledge of plants, and especially to adapt convenient windows for their cultivation.

In the City and Countryside

Years ago, I didn't know that certain plants, with a little care and attention, might be made to grow in windows where the straggling rays of light are toned down to a dingy hue. Had I known I could create something, in a cramped city, as well as a tended garden in a large country home, I would have undertaken this task that much quicker.

Spring flowers in the woods - Image: Becky

The greatest doubt I have is to be able to persuade some who are very dubious on the subject to begin the cultivation of window-plants those who can see no beauty in the quiet enjoyment of relaxing in their homes on a sofa or armchair by their own window, rather than head out onto the town for enjoyment. Fortunately there are lots of homebodies out there who also fancy gardening, and my writing this was buoyed by the thought that my little book may be of some service to those aspiring to the pursuit of floriculture as a recreation.

Under present circumstances, the artisan, or humble florist, however much they may have the love of flowers at heart, is much restrained in his ambition to grow a few plants, from the fact that his window affords little scope for their cultivation.

At the best the cultivators of window- plants have but room for two or three specimens, which are either placed on the window sill, or on brackets higher up the window, circumstances which almost bid defiance to any training of a plant except a one-sided specimen. Then, again, the plants are continually receiving the dust of the household, which, combined with the full glare of gas by night, very soon brings the plants to assume a sickly appearance, entailing considerable care and attention on the part of the cultivator to keep them in a healthy condition. That being the case, it is not to be wondered at why the cultivators of window-plants proceed with the pursuit in a blow hot, blow cold sort of way. When the markets are teeming with the attributes of spring, they are induced to purchase a plant or two. Exultingly the plants are carried home, assigned the sunniest place in the window, and duly killed with kindness, the window remaining for the rest of the season without a semblance of vegetation.

Therefore, the horticulturist who would cater to spread a taste for window gardening, ought to have his attention arrested by these existing circumstances, and besides giving the household florist a knowledge how to grow the plants he seeks to cultivate, it would be well at the same time to show him some construction of the window which would give greater facilities to the cultivation of plants, and also obviate some of the drawbacks mentioned. This I have endeavored to do by bringing before your notice the window or miniature greenhouse, which will not only be found admirably adapted for the cultivation of a few plants all the year round, but also an ornament to the mansion as well as the house or the apartment. The miniature greenhouse will be found more convenient and better adapted for growing plants than either the aquarium or the glass shade, which are continually in the way, and require great attention in keeping clean and fit to be looked at.

An exterior window box - Image: Spencer Means

But the greenhouse being attached to the outside of the window is out of the way. Not only that, but the plants get more air; they are easier examined, and more securely shut off from odors and dust of the household. Besides, the miniature greenhouse, when adorned with a few plants, would mend the prospect of many a dwelling by blocking out offensive objects, which is certainly not the least of its advantages.

Window garden in London, overlooking the Thames - Image: Steve Daniels

Window boxes have long enjoyed use, having originated in the countryside but spread to the cities. Recent decades, as the proportion of humanity living in urban areas grows ever higher, have triggered a greater uptake. It is common now, when walking the street en route to work or the store, to behold a beautiful few specimens.

Then, too, as if not to be behind the blackbird, would the plants in the little greenhouse seem to dance to the beat of the hammer. I was just chin-tall enough for the windowsill, and to my young mind what mystery hung around that fairy-looking dwelling, into which I earnestly gazed. And although no impulse was awakened within me to inquire of the shoemaker how he came to think of his little greenhouse, or where he had drawn his pattern from, yet impressions were indelibly made.

And now, in looking back through the telescope of the mind, those impressions, like a far-off landscape, become distinctly visible the shoemaker, the blackbird, and the little greenhouse, stands out in bold relief. And where was this little greenhouse, think you? It was attached to the outside-of a back window five stories high. And whether it was intended to shut out offensive objects, or as a hobby, it is no matter; there it was, giving pleasure to the shoemaker, who to my imagination was the happiest man on earth. I even went so far as to say that I myself would be a shoemaker, and have a blackbird and a little greenhouse. But somehow or other the garments of the mind are easier to change than those of the body ; and when it became time for me to leave school, which was no sooner than I wanted, the happy shoemaker and his dwelling gave way to objects of a more exciting nature.

Some will think that certain professionals who work with their hands are better adapted to the art of window gardening; that those without such a hands-on vocation are at a great disadvantage. Others still give up at the first hurdle; on seeing plants droop, so they themselves droops and give up hope, thinking that the plants could not sustain life from the attention they could give them. That's a false fear begotten from hesitation, which if suffered to remain corrodes the best of intentions. Plants will sustain life wonderfully with but little attention, even they themselves will struggle for an existence, and it is only when we become unnatural or reckless in our treatment of them that they sometimes leave us.

I have seen plants in some windows where I could have burst into the house and gone to work for the sake of those plants by washing off the dust which had accumulated on their leaves; others I could have put away in some out-of-the-way corner, quietly to rest for a season, being well assured, when awakened, they would bud, shoot and bloom with double vigor.

A solitary plant at the window - Image: Theornamentalist

I have also noticed the uncomfortable position of plants in a great many windows. And when I have seen them with their leaves pressed hard against the window frames, I have always been reminded of a boy pressing his nose against the window of a candy shop, as eager to get in as the plants were to get out. You may be sure, that when the leaves of the plant are pressing against the window, that the habit of the plant is spoiling fast; the leaves which lean against the glass not only hurt themselves, but they also prevent the light from reaching other parts of the plant, which in the struggle to be as near the light as their neighbors become very much attenuated, presenting plenty of leaves to the passer-by, but nothing but long, bare, wiry-looking branches to the cultivator. Now if those plants had been turned round now and then, so as to expose every part of the plant successively to the light, the branches would have become nicely balanced, and the outline of the plants would have been ad- mired as much as the skill of the cultivator.

An acquaintance of mine had a plant which hung from the roof and which possessed great attraction for me. This plant had roundish, bronzy-green, hairy-looking leaves, and it threw out a number of red-like threads, which hung down over the sides of the pot and to the extremity of each a little plant was attached; then there were two or three other plants which rested on the bottom of the little greenhouse, strange, dumpy looking fellows, all prickles and points, and very seldom seen among the fashionable plants of the present day. The shoemaker, I will remember, called the one which was sus- pended from the roof "Aaron's Beard." The others were one or two sorts of cacti, and a variegated aloe, all of which I have since learned will grow in the same flower-pot for years and require but little attention beyond being kept clean, and receiving a little water during the summer season.

As there are hundreds of plants quite suitable for window culture, the plan adopted in the following pages will be found to meet the requirements of all classes. Beside explaining the construction of the miniature greenhouse, and how to make certain window garden displays where the aid of the greenhouse is not available calculated for the cultivation of plants, they will also show how each may be adorned with a few inexpensive plants in spring, summer, autumn and winter. When these are done with, we examine how a few varieties of choicer, costlier and more challenging yet beautiful plants can succeed them.

Having offered these few introductory hints on Window Gardening, I trust that my unpretending little work on this, one of the simplest modes of cultivating flowers, may find favor and indulgence from those who, like myself, cherish a warm affection for these precious things. Whether you have a scanty amount of space or by necessity dwell in the confined streets of the metropolis or other large towns, it is difficult to gratify a taste more pure and elevating as growing flowers.

Window Greenhouses, Window Boxes & Window Awnings

This chapter offers a simple means of constructing a little window greenhouse. Although such a contraption isn't necessary for window gardening, it can greatly attenuate the sunlight and warmth which plants, be they ferns or flowering, enjoy all year round. Intended to slot into windows which slide upward, this design is affixed to a window in a way to afford more exterior shelf space, being sturdier and safer than a simple overhanging planter. Be sure to work and proportion these instructions to the measurements of the window you are working with; ordinary plywood suffices for this project.

You will perceive that the picture does not interfere with the sliding of the window-sashes, and that the ventilation of the dwelling and greenhouse are independent of each other. This should be maintained whatever modification the little conservatory may undergo. My window is 5 feet high and 3 1-2 feet broad, and the greenhouse attached to it is 3 feet high and 2 1-2 feet broad, with a front elevation of 2 feet.

The ventilator at the top of the greenhouse is merely a piece of board, hinged to the back piece, and held open by means of a little hook and staple. In order that a constant stream of air may be passing through the structure, several little holes are pierced in the bottom, which may be covered or left uncovered at pleasure. The whole, except the bottom, is firmly dovetailed together, and secured to the window in the following manner:

To each side of the window, and the outside, and close to the windowsill, is fixed an upright board, three-quarters of an inch thick, and broad enough to lie flush with the outer face of the wall. These uprights are made more secure by means of a cross batten at the top, which should be made to fit as tight as possible, and be well driven home. Two brackets," with projecting arms of two feet, for the green- house to rest upon, are screwed to the bottom sill of the window.

Mini greenhouse - Image: Rebecca Partington

This being done, the greenhouse is lifted on to the brackets and screwed to them, also to the uprights, which, it must be remembered, are part of the breadth of the greenhouse. Therefore an allowance for them must be made accordingly.

If all the foregoing details are done in a workmanlike manner, the stoutest gale will never disturb the miniature greenhouse. But if you cannot construct it yourself, any respectable joiner can help you put together such a one as I have described, at a reasonable price. You can also buy, from large garden stores, premade devices which more than adequately fulfil a purpose.

Houses with bow-windows seem to me to be well adapted for the cultivation of flowers. And where the recess could be spared, the bow-window, with little expense, might be converted into an elegant little greenhouse: For such a purpose all that is required is merely a little wooden or wire stage for the plants to stand upon, and a curtain hanging square with the room, to shut the plants off' at night from the gaseous air, or when dusting the apartment. The stage might be constructed in the following manner:

The shelf of the stage should be about two feet from the floor, and placed so that one end would be at the center of the window, and the other nearly square with the room. The other shelves of the stage should rise by steps from the center one, to each side of the window. One center shelf, with three or four others running from it to each side of the window, would give the cultivator space for the purpose of growing a number of plants. And by constructing the stage in this manner, the apartment would not be so much darkened as if the plants were allowed to stand fair before the window.

No doubt some people are to be found altogether against having plants in the window, from the very reason that the already dark apartment would be darker still. But would this darkness, dreaded by them, not be akin to the sweet gloom of the forest; or again, if the windows were full of the noonday sun, would it not be better to let the fierce rays of that luminary be subdued by flickering into the dwelling through graceful fronds and fragrant flowers, than drawing blinds, however beautiful they might be? What artificial blind could be compared to that natural one, which presents such a boundless field for change and recreation?

With regard to window-boxes, a great many people secure no little pleasure in growing a few flowers in boxes placed outside of the window, and that enjoyment might be increased greatly by protecting the flowers from the scorching heat of the sun and heavy rains. And for that purpose we have only to copy the store owner in his efforts to prevent the sun from spoiling the wares in his windows. How much more comfortable the plants would feel, we need hardly say, while in these extremities, to be under the protection of a little canopy?

For this, all that would be required might be had for a small sum.

A roller with a chintz blind, fixed half way up the window, and two projecting rods, just above the flowers, with a piece of cord through the end of each, to draw down the blind, with the common window-blind fixture to draw it up, and the job is complete. The drawing down of the blind of an evening, and in cold weather in early spring, would greatly prosper the establishment of spring-flowering bulbs, bringing them into flower much sooner, and also making them last longer. And by the same economy the season of summer-flowering plants would be materially lengthened and extended into late autumn advantages which speak loudly in favor of giving flowers in window-boxes that simple, yet efficient, protection.

But, after all, my favorite is the miniature greenhouse, possessing, as it does, great advantages, over all other appliances for window gardening. And when it is got up neatly, and nicely painted, using good plain glass, the little structure embellishes the habitation wonderfully.

In some residences where the apartments are heated by hot water apparatus, I see nothing to prevent the miniature greenhouse from being heated by the same means. Hot water can be laid almost anywhere by experienced workmen, and a couple of inch pipes led round the bottom of the greenhouse, would give sufficient heat to resist a great amount of frost, and thus some of the more choice green house, if not stove plants, might be cultivated. With reference to dwellings of the working classes, the builders of cottage properties might, by introducing the miniature greenhouse on finishing the house, obtain more rent, and also be the means of leading the dwellers into a more happy and contented kind of life. What a contrast to the existing state of things, when their happiness, as it were, passes through a sieve shaken by their own hands, leaving nothing but lumps of sorrow for the rest of their clays. At any rate, the principle is worth trying.

How cheerful it is to pass along a street where the houses have small gardens in front, and to see in the windows of those houses a fuchsia or a geranium striving to catch a glimpse of the sun. What a heightened tone it would give to the picture to introduce a miniature greenhouse, gaily dressed with some of nature's simplest but sweetest gems.

We can find a type for us all among the flowers. If we wish to be proud, we have only to cultivate the poppy. But if we wish to live and be respected, let us be mindful of the daisy, the primrose, and the snowdrop. The last three live in melody of song. Here is the rhyme that measures the poppy:

"Pleasures are like poppies spread,

You seize the flower, the bloom is fled."

To resume more practical matter let me say, that with the miniature greenhouse, and a modest sum each year spare for flowers, the household florist need never be without a plant in flower any week of the year. It is even wonderful what a display of flowers can be had, as I will show, for a small price. But before proceeding with what to grow and how to grow, a few remarks relating to plant life in general will not be out of place, which leads us to our next chapter.

How to Keep Window Plants Healthy

As with keeping yourself clean, plant cleanliness is essential to healthiness. Therefore, whatever plants may be growing in the window, the dust of the dwelling must not be allowed to accumulate on their leaves week after week; they should be carefully washed every now and then with a sponge and a little tepid water.

An aphid; one of the most destructive plant pests - Image: MedievalRich

In doing this, do not take hold of the leaf with the fingers as with a pair of pincers, but let the footstalk of the leaf slip in between the fingers of the left hand, and the back of the leaf lie on the palm of the hand. Then apply the sponge until the leaf be properly cleansed. In sponging the feathery fronds of ferns the task is rather more delicate. Let a portion of the frond lie on the palm of the hand, and with the sponge moderately wet, press the frond against the hand gently, but do not rub the sponge up and down, and shifting the hand forward with the operation until the frond is finished.

This sponging is to keep the leaf free from dust, and to wash any scaly insects from off the leaves, or fronds. These insects generally lodge on the back of the leaves, near to the midrib, and should have no quarter whatever from the cultivator. There is also another insect commonly called the aphid, which is a great pest to certain plants, and if suffered to remain, will wholly ruin the plants. Spring-flowering plants, such as the calceolaria and cineraria, are particularly subject to this annoyance; also the show geraniums and the young shoots of the fuchsia, as well as many other soft-wooded plants are infested with this fly. The species being rapidly propagated, the insect should be destroyed immediately on being detected, and for this the sponge is of no avail.

The best and surest way of destruction is to fumigate the plants infected with pure tobacco smoke. The non-smoker may do this very effectually in the following manner: With the stalk or runt of a cabbage, or any similar object, make a sort of horn, and fix the narrow end on the nozzle of the tire bellows. Then push a little shag tobacco into the horn, and place a small, red-hot cinder on the top of it, and a little more tobacco on the cinder, and with the ventilators of the greenhouse shut, and the window down to the mouth of the horn, blow the bellows until the greenhouse is densely full of smoke, in which state it should remain for two or three hours.

When the smoke has cleared away examine the plants, and if the fumigation has done its work, the insects will be lying on their backs on the leaves and roundabout, perhaps not dead, but so as they can be easily shook or blown from the plants. After that has been done, sweep the remains into the dust-pan, and the execution is completed.

Those who have not the advantage of the miniature green- house must devise some other means to retain the smoke round about the plant. An empty box or a large paper bag to envelop the plant would be equally suitable.

After fumigation and the insects are cleared away, the plants, if not in flower, might receive a gentle watering over head with advantage.

Thus far I have shown how to keep plants healthy by keeping them clean. Let us see what else they require to keep them in that state: Air, food, light, training, and rest. I might have included the first two under food alone; but it suits the present purpose better for them to be separated. To keep plants pent up for weeks and months without any air but what comes bouncing in when the door is opened, or whistling through the keyhole when closed, is not the way to keep plants healthy.

All our hardy ferns, all spring-flowering plants, all summer geraniums and autumn chrysanthemums, love to feel the freshness of the air; in fact, it is their very life. And although the freshness of the air may be said to be very seldom abroad in our large towns, yet, by keeping the leaves of the plants clean, they are the more able to breathe of what is going; but they must first have the opportunity of doing so, and that frequently, to keep them healthy. We now come to the food of plants soil and water.

It cannot be expected that window-gardeners are able to pay the same attention to the food of plants as is practiced by professional gardeners; though I must say, all books hitherto written for the guidance of amateur gardeners would lead one to think otherwise. Now, in the matter of soil and water soil especially we know that the amateur is placed at a very great disadvantage in comparison with the professional gardener; and to recommend certain strictness, or the plants will not grow, is quite out of character.

It is quite true that certain plants require a certain soil to grow in and be well; in fact, we see that in nature. On the other hand, it is as true that we see miscellaneous plants growing in what may be termed miscellaneous soil. Therefore, to meet the case of the window-gardener, the better plan would be to adapt the circumstances to the man, not the man to the circumstances, by giving him a certain soil for a number of plants, and by telling him to water the plants when dry, be it morning, noon, or night, unless when the plants are at rest.

A soil which would be the most suitable and the most easily obtained for all window-plants to grow in, can be found in any locality where there is a hedge growing. Go along the side of the hedge by the roadside, and pull up the first big tuft of grass, and shake the soil from it and add a handful or two of sand(silver-sand, if possible, bought at a seed shop), and the mixture will suit almost any window- plant requiring soil for its cultivation. An even easier plan would be to visit the garden center for some sandy, loamy soil. A single bag of this should suffice for filling all your planters and pots, with the cost not running too high for such a sack.

The operation of potting will be treated in a subsequent chapter; but I may here mention that good drainage placed in the bottom of the flower-pot, so that the water may run freely away from the soil, and the soil put down equally round about the roots, and to be of one uniform firmness, are the chief and successful features in potting all plants. Giving the plants good drainage, and a nice sandy loam to grow in, counteracts the evils arising from the plants getting too much water, to which window plants are commonly subjected, and are thereby rendered unhealthy, from the soil becoming sour.

In fact, this plan is adopted by some garden centers in order to prevent the same evil; which fact I learned in the following manner I went to browse said garden center, and one morning a miscellaneous collection of plants was pointed out to me which required re-potting.

Relying confidently on my own notions, I cast my eyes over the plants, and proceeded to the potting shed to prepare the soil, etc., thinking in my mind that I would make the plants comfortable for once. So I hurried away with the barrow for a bit of this soil and a bit of that. My good intentions were checked rather abruptly by the store manager telling me to give the plants all one soil, and be sure to put plenty of sand into it; "for," says he, " our guys are very careless in watering the plants, or whether they want to or not."

In spring and summer, however willing (sometimes they might be more so), they have not time to examine the plants minutely, and for the sake of expedition, water the plants without due care, straight forward, one by one.

Thus it was that I got the cue about putting plenty of sand in the soil, and in these days of special manures, which give such miraculous results, the sandy soil can be easily enriched by the application of some of those fertilizers; for instance, a handful of Peruviau guano, dissolved in water, and given to the plants about once a week, in the growing season, would promote a healthy vigor in the plants. In potting plants, be careful to cast out any worms, however small, from the soil, for if potted with the plant, the worms will soon become a great fact, twisting in all directions about the root, beside living on the fat of the soil, which is very hurtful to the health of the plant.

Just fancy having the naked foot in a peck of soil, and a long worm twisting between the toes, and having no power to prevent the gyrations of the tormentor. I have heard people claim, when some of the window plants have been doing badly, "I'm sure there's a worm at the root of that plant;" but they have done nothing to ascertain the fact.

Thus the plants have gone on in this state for months. To ascertain whether there be a worm at the root of the plant or not, turn the plant upside down, with the neck of the plant between the ringers of the left hand, and the right hand on the bottom of the pot, give the edge of the pot a tap or two on the window sill, and the ball of soil containing the roots will come out. If the fancied worm is there, several little channels will be made all round the sides of the ball, and, perhaps, the maker will be coiled into a lump close to the side.

Fork him out at once, and fill up any vacancies with a little fresh soil. In re-potting the plant, give the bottom of the pot a tap or two on the floor, to settle the ball nicely down. If no channels or little holes are visible on the sides of the ball, it is safe to conclude there is no worm, and the unhealthiness of the plant must arise from other causes.

With respect to watering plants the position of the miniature greenhouse, and windows in general, being a dry one in summer, the plants will require to be almost daily watered, and all soft-wooded plants before coming into flower, are much benefited by having their leaves well besprinkled with clean water, two or three times a week, or more often if possible.

This brings us to the training; as the child requires training, so does the plant. Plants of the geranium type should never be suffered to become leggy, that is, possessing long, bare branches with a few green leaves on the top.

Endeavor to keep the plant as bushy as possible, and near to the pot, letting no branch have preponderance over another. This is accomplished by nipping off the points of the young shoots after the plant has been potted in spring, and made some progress in growing; also, by leading branches into any weak side of the plant. Nipping the points of the young shoots induces the plant to throw out numerous other shoots, hence the practice. More information on the training of plants will be found further on, in the chapter describing the cultivation of the fuchsia.

A simple plastic watering can is all that's necessary for watering - Image: DonBanana

We now come to the rest of plants. The natural rest of plants is discernible in some, while in others it is more obscure. Thus we see the trees of the forest, the hedge-rows, and the fruit-trees of our gardens lose their leaves and go quietly to sleep. The rough winds may try to shake them from their lethargy. But it is not until the sweet voice of spring calling melodiously for leafy boughs, that the sleepers are necessitated to awake and fulfil the divine mission of love. Then away they burst, leading forth a glorious sound to nature's choristers.

Nearly all plants under pot culture require rest in due sea- son, and that season i3 generally after the plants have done flowering. All plants that have flowered during summer, such as the geraniums of sorts, aud fuchsias, are rested by being kept moderately dry at the roots all through the winter. In fact the fuchsia should be taken out of the win- dow altogether in that season, and placed away in some dry cellar or shelf, free from frost, to remain there until spring comes round.

The plant is then brought forth, and the shoots shortened, the roots shaken out of the old soil, and re-potted in fresh, set in the window, and away the plant goes on the journey of life. Just like the laborer, who, having gone through the operation of the toilet, after a good night's sleep, marches off to his work with renewed vigor; requiring wholesome food and cleanly habits to keep him healthy, and we may add content, to make him happy.

Thus we see to keep a window-plant healthy, the leaves of the plant must be kept clean; they must have plenty of air, and abundance of water be given to the plant during the growing season, which must be potted in a nice free sandy soil, well-drained, and now and then receive a little liquid manure.

The plant must also be trained by pinching off the points of the young shoots, or tying them down; and whether or not the plant has fulfilled its task by shedding a few flowers, the plant must have a little rest after its exertions, which will be noticed in the remarks on the cultivation of plants in the succeeding chapters.

Ferns

Among the many varieties of wild plants that grow around our cities, or far away in the country, none seem more interesting than the fern tribe. Indeed, I may say that none are better adapted for decorating the miniature greenhouse.

Kimberly Queen Fern - Image: Erusalio

Their graceful fronds, like palms in miniature, are more lasting, if they are not so pretty, as the blossom of the primrose; and although the greater number of the varieties of ferns love shady nooks, yet there are some varieties that grow far up on the hills, where they receive little or no shelter from the scorching rays of the sun, nor does the hardest winter nip their lonely fronds. Therefore, our windows being furnished with the miniature greenhouse, whether they partake of the dull aspect of the back slums or the hot and dusty thoroughfare, may be adorned and made cheerful by a few objects drawn from that part of nature's boundless store. It is not my intention to give a long list of varieties to choose from that would be but to confuse you with a host of hard botanical names which the daisy, the buttercup and the fern knew not until science christened them afresh; but to confine my remarks to a few varieties of ferns and other wild plants which grow in almost every country; also a few cultivated plants. And for the guidance of those persons who may have some difficulty in getting to the places where the wild plants grow, I will, at the close of my remarks, add a list of the whole, with their prices affixed, and which can be purchased from any garden center.

The first family or tribe of ferns that I would draw your attention to as being worthy of notice is the "Hart's tongue," or Scolopendrium vulgare, of botanists. In searching for this fern, remember that it will be found growing most luxuriantly by the side of brooks in deep glens, where the spray of the brook leaps up and kisses it in gratitude for its company. I think that it would be cruel to part such sweet friends; nay, the plant would pine away in absence of the brook. See, there is one of the same kind a little higher up the bank, more likely to live with you; for now that plants, when transplanted from very sheltered places, from being tender, are more liable to die than others taken from exposed situations. This is a great lesson on plant cultivation.

And here let me say that if you wish the plants which you gather from their wild homes "to do well with you, you must not be like some cruel plant-seekers, who, in the most ruthless manner, tear them away from the soil in which they are found growing, and tumble them into a handkerchief, and by the time they reach home their lovely fronds are all bruised and broken. When you espy one which you would like, you must go to work systematically.

Having armed yourself with a little trowel, and a longish tin box slung from your shoulder, stoop down and examine the plant carefully. If it be that the roots of the plant are fast embedded in stones, look for another that is less so; tie up the leaves or fronds with a piece of band, and loosen the soil round about it with the trowel. Be careful in doing so not to come any nearer the plant than three inches, and preserve, if possible, every portion of rootlet intact. When you have got the plant up, you may reduce the ball of soil considerably, and put the plant gently into your gathering container.

The Scolopendrium grows in tufts, and in favored situations throws out numerous dark-green colored shining fronds, varying from eight inches to two feet in length, ac- cording to the locality. The fronds are of a stiffish, leathery nature, slightly curved, and varying in breadth, but two inches at the broadest part, which is a little beyond the middle of the frond, may be taken as an average ; then they gradually taper to a point; from the same part they gradually decline in breadth to within six inches of the crown of the plant, where the leafy portion of the frond abruptly terminates in a heart-shaped manner, and the whole is supported on a stout, dark-brown colored stalk or stipe.

This stipe immediately joins the frond, and is termed the " mid-rib," and partakes more of the green color of the frond on the upper surface, but on the under it retains the dark color of the stipe nearly throughout. On the underside of the fronds a number of broad, parallel lines, covered, in a mature state, with a brown sort of dust, stand out in oblique directions with the mid-rib very prominently. All ferns, with a few exceptions, like the Scolopendrium, are marked in various manners on the underside of the fronds.

The Asplenium scolopendrium, or Scolopendrium vulgare - Image: H. Zell

These marks botanists call son", and constitute, so to speak, the flower of the fern; and from their position and formation the different tribes of ferns are partly distinguished. It is not from any fancied resemblance to the colored petals of a flower that those marks are considered as the flower of the fern, but simply from the fact that it is there that the seed of the future plant is developed. That brown dust, which becomes almost invisible when separated from its kindred, to become a living plant, might we not say here is life almost from nothingness.

Beside the Scolopendrium vulgare, there are a great many very interesting varieties one garden center advertising near upon a hundred different sorts. But there are only two or three to be found in a state of wildness, and those nut near so common as vulgare. That, and the two following varieties, may be said to be chief of the species found in a wild state.

Scolo'pendrium crispum is readily distinguished from vulgare, by having the edge of the fronds frilled much after the fashion of the shirt front of former days, and which some of our grandfathers still stick to with great tenacity. Indeed, if the fronds of this variety were of a glossy white instead of a light glossy green, they would be a capital imitation and no doubt nature, in the first instance, as she does in many more, furnished the design of the frilled front.

Scolopendrium cristatum is easily distinguished from the foregoing varieties by having the tips of the fronds crumpled, like so many green tassels waving in the wiud. This variety, as well as that of crispuni, displays a great craving for admiration, and therefore oughtto find a corner in the miniature greenhouse. The filled and crested varieties are barren of fructification; that is to say, they have no patches of so?*i on the fronds. The reason of their barrenness is imperfectly known; but it is supposed that, like a great many more higher up in the scale .of nature, who see no efficacy in hidden beauty, therefore expose all to the first glance. But it would be well if they imitated this little fern, and exposed nothing but their own ware.

The name 'Scolopendrium," which is applied to this genus of ferns, is supposed to have been given to it by botanists from the resemblance which the sort bears to the feet of the centipede, or " Jenny-with-the-hundred-feet," which is scientifically termed Scolopendra or otherwise Scolopendrium. But I can see no likeness between the two, unless it be the fancied resemblance which the oblong patch of brown sort bears to the insect itself.

The aspect of these three varieties of ferns, taken in the order treated of, is the simplest in the whole genera of British ferns from the circumstance that their fronds are more entire than all other species; that is, they are not cut up into numerous wings or pinnoe, which give to other ferns a feathery appearance.

Blechnum, or 'hard ferns' - Image: Franz Xaver

The northern hard fern, or common hard fern, or Blechnum boreale of botanists, is the next fern to which I would call your attention. It may be said to be the only wild variety that we possess belonging to that interesting group of ferns; though sometimes, in the search for this fern, we may come across a decided sport that is, a variety with characteristics quite different from the common variety. I've gathered specimens of the Blechnum with the fronds more or less forked at the point, like a fish-tail. The place where I gathered that singular sport was on the bank of a country lane, where I have also gathered specimens of the common variety, with fertile mm is two feet five inches in length, having barren fronds nearly two feet. I never saw the common hard fern grow so luxuriantly as it does in that lane; and in the present season that is, the month of October the fronds literally clothe the bank with robes of glossy green, when all around is brown and sere.

Here, then, we may say that these ferns have been growing from time immemorial; and in examining the soil in which they are growing, we find it to be composed wholly of decayed vegetable matter, not boggy, but leafy and loose. And in looking at the position of the bank, with an aspect almost due west, slightly shaded by trees, one would almost think that the ferns would suffer greatly in the hot summer months.

But such is not the case. The roots being well covered with their own decayed fronds and other grassy matter, are always in a most healthy state; but take away that covering for a summer's day, and the fronds would become shrivelled and brown long before their season, which you would do well to remember. And as we cannot suffer decayed fronds to remain about the plants, from their unsightliness, other means must be devised which would secure the same ends. A little moss would answer the purpose, and look well at the same time. And if little round baskets, also covered with moss, could be procured to place the flower-pots in the whole ends would be obtained.

The common hard fern grows in tufts similar to the hart's tongue, and is possessed of two different kinds of fronds, namely, barren and fertile ones. The former are evergreen, almost prostrate, and of various lengths, from one inch to three inches at their broadest part, and from six inches to twenty inches may be taken as their length.

The lower portion of the frond is pinnate, while the upper is "pinnatind;" that is, the leafy portion of the frond commencing at the stipe is cut completely away at intervals varying in breadth according to the size of the frond, and toward the apex of the frond it is only partially cut, not fully reaching to the mid- rib; and the whole aspect of the frond is what is termed “lanceolate," or spear-shaped. The fertile fronds, spring up from the root a little later on in the season. They are more erect and somewhat taller, but narrower in front and in pinnae than the barren ones. They are not strictly evergreen, and on the underside of the pinnae, along each side of the mid-vein with the sort, is exposed to view, a longitudinal patch, similar to the hart's tongue, but darker in color. The fertile as well as the barren fronds are supported on very dark-colored stipes, which have a little groove or channel running the entire length of the frond on the upper surface.

Toward the root the stipes are covered with a scaly sort of substance, and both fronds are extremely hard to the touch; hence the very appropriate name, common “hard fern."

I have now explained, as well as I know how, in plain language, the chief characteristics of the foregoing ferns, and would willingly continue further afield; but that field is so wide and full of objects, that I am almost placed in the same predicament as the lady who had a thousand dresses to choose from, and who was under the painful necessity of frittering away the greater part of the "day in considering which to put on ; and who, when dressed, had sometimes no little mortification in thinking that she might have looked much better in something else.

Though I have had a good deal of frittering to do in choosing the wherewithal to dress the miniature greenhouse, yet I hope to have none of that lady's mortification; but, before stepping away from the ferns of our woods, let me point out, in the next chapter, another group as being well worthy of attention.

Wild Ferns

The common poly pod, or Polypodium vidgare of botanists. The word " vulgare" which requires the final " e" to be sounded, is very often applied scientifically to plants to denote that they are common, just as the word vulgar is commonly applied to individuals who are rude and boorish in their manners, and common enough they are. But the sense in each case is rather different. If it were applied to man- kind with the same meaning as is attached to the little fern, we should all be vulgar, which is too sweeping a conclusion ; and it would be a great pity if the fern could mend its commonness, but a great blessing it the majority of men would mend their manners.

Polypodium vulgare - Image: BerndH

The common polypod is a fern that adapts itself, and makes the most of the various situations in which it may be found growing; sometimes waving its pale, green-colored fronds by the wayside; sometimes by the brook; now hanging over the abyss of the quarry, and often bidding defiance to the storm on the high rocks of the hills. What a lesson might be read from the adaptability of this little fern. In describing the Polypodium vulgare, I must call your attention to a part of the plant on which I have hitherto been silent, namely, a certain part of the root, which is a distinct feature in this fern, and more or less of all the other varieties that compose the group of polypods. Wherever growing,

the stipes of the common polypods will be found to spring from a number of brown, hairy-like feet, which are called "rhizomes," and which creep along the top, and also spread under the ground. In fact, the name polypodium, which is derived from the Greek, signifies many-footed, and in some foreign or exotic varieties those hairy creeping stems are not unlike a foot of a hare; in fact, it is sometimes called the hare's foot fern.

The "rhizomes," or creeping stems of the common polypody, are from a quarter to half an inch in diameter, and in a young state are covered with a light-brown chaffy sub- stance, which gives them the appearance of being covered with hair. Through course of time they partly lose that hairiness, and are sometimes completely covered with black rootlets, which penetrate or ramify into the crevices of rocks, decayed trunks of trees, and other surfaces suitable for their support.

The fronds rising in all directions from the young rhizomes give this fern quite a different aspect from the tufted habit of the hart's tongue. The fronds are of a pale-green color, growing from nine to eighteen inches high, and are supported on short wiry-looking stipes. The outline of the frond is lanceolate, and the leafy portion is divided into segments much after the manner of the common hard fern, and called pinnatifid. On the underside of those divisions, toward the upper half of the frond, the sori appearing in a very regular manner, little brown, lozenge-like spots being arranged, single tile, on each side of the mid-vein, and the indentations of these little spots are easily seen on the upper surface of the frond.

This fern is common across Western Europe and the USA. In sheltered places the fronds are evergreen, and can be readily distinguished from all other native ferns, from the manner of their fructification, combined with the hairy- creeping rhizome. There are two other varieties which are, perhaps, more worthy of attention than Polypodium vulgare.

But they are not so easily found: one is chiefly confined to the mountains and the other to low grounds. The former is called Polypodium cambricum, and has a more leafy appear- ance than the vulgare ; but it is quite barren of sori. The other is called Polypodium semilacerum, and it resembles cambricum ; with this difference, that the upper half of the fronds are generally fertile.

Varieties of Ferns for the Miniature Greenhouse

For those who may desire something better than ordinary sorts by way of ferns, the following choice varieties will be found a decided acquisition for embellishing the miniature greenhouse. The first claiming special attention is named Lastrea cristata, or crested buckler fern.

This variety throws out several fronds from two to four feet in length, gracefully rising from a dark, scaly, tree-like stem. The edges of the deep green-colored fronds being beautifully crested, give this fern an elegance unsurpassed by any other varieties of hardy ferns; and where a noble and striking specimen is desired, Lastrea cristata should be remembered.

Close-up of a buckler fern - Image: Rosser1954

As a contrast to the foregoing variety in habit and color, Pulypodium auritum, or eared polypody, may be favorably mentioned; the fronds being a pale green color, and erect, bushy habit, breaks, but does not obscure the wavy outline of the Lastrea. Another great favorite which would nearly correspond with the two foregoing ferns is named Adiantum capillas veneris, or the maiden-hair fern.

So delicate is this little fern in the structure of the fronds and lilies, and gracefulness of habit, combined with the refreshing greenness which the leaflets possess, as to entitle this fern to a prominent position in all collections. With the Lastrea cristata as a back- ground, and the Polypodium auritum placed in front, with the maiden-hair in front of that, a beautiful bank of ferns is formed; and when a pan of moss is placed before the ferns, the group is worthy the pencil of the artist.

Cultivating Ferns

The foregoing varieties of ferns, as well as many more beside, may be easily grown by giving them a little shelter from the hot summer sun, and by keeping drought from their roots; they will well repay any other little attention bestowed. The varieties before mentioned will also be found to luxuriate most in a loose, leafy soil, with a good sprinkling of silver-sand, and when grown in pots, nature must be imitated as nearly as possible.

On woody banks the soil can never become sour and unhealthy from being waterlogged. Though some ferns are found growing with great strength by the side of brooks, where the soil is natu- rally wet, yet that circumstance will be found to be a sweet dampness. The ferns in such situations have, as it were, a fresh mouthful of food every instant of the day, and their appetite is increased by inhaling the pure air of the forest. Only let the brook become a muddy pool, shut up in a greenhouse with the same ferns, growing as in a state of nature, and what would be the result? The vigor of the fronds for want of fresh air would become languid, and then a prey to all sorts of insects; while the rootlets under the double disadvantage of sour food and flaccid fronds would, in a measure, be choked.

Thus the process of destruction would be going on at both ends, and if the plant did not actually die, a much different habit would supervene. Or take it in another way. Let the plants have abundance of fresh air, and yet be planted in the muddy pool, what then would be the result?

However wantonly the breeze might woo their lovely fronds, the roots would have no better action than in the former case.

Their sour food would still make them less eager for work, and instead of extending to a numerous progeny the plant would eventually, if left to nature, fall before the rush and the water flag in the struggle for existence. To cultivate the plant so would be to cultivate it against nature; and all the coaxing in the world would never be crowned with successful cultivation, unless the roots also came jn for a fair share of attention, and that attention can be summed up in a very few words plenty of drainage to prevent the soil from becoming sour like that of the stagnant pool.

Fanners know the utility of good drainage; and however ridiculous it may appear to some people to talk about draining a flower-pot, yet gardeners know, or ought to know, that that operation is as necessary for the well-being of a plant, as it is for the produce of the farm. The operation is not only necessary for ferns, but likewise for all plants under pot culture. Therefore I will endeavor to show you bow to proceed in that operation, also how to pot the ferns, and other details connected with their cultivation.

Gardeners in pots and plants are always careful to cover the hole in the bottom of the flower-pot with a good sized piece of broken earthenware called a crock, and the process crocking; then on the top of that they place a handful or two of smaller pieces, and over all a little moss to prevent the soil from choking up the drainage.

As gardeners generally have plenty of broken flower-pots they are used up for this purpose; but as you may not be desirous to break a new flower-plot, or even a dish, though it be cracked, a few oyster shells will do equally well; and that is all which they consider necessary beyond soil, a little water now and then, and plenty of air to keep the roots in a healthy condition. In proceeding further to pot the plant, whether it be a fern, a primrose, a geranium, or a fuchsia, or, indeed, with hundreds of others beside, a sufficient soil is put into the pot, so that when gently pressed down, it will sup- port the ball of roots, and allow the stem of the plant, at about an inch above the root, to be on a level with the brim of the pot.

The stem should rise from the center of the pot, and the pot should be large enough to admit at least an inch of soil between its sides and the ball of roots. The soil is pressed down with the fingers, sometimes with a little stick when the pot is a very deep one, but in all cases the soil is made of one uniform firmness round the roots of the plant, and I was going to say, levelled down to within half an inch of the brim of the pot, but this last process must depend very much upon the size of the pot; however, that distance will suit whatever is cultivated in the miniature greenhouse.

After potting any of the ferns which I already pointed out, whether collected in spring, summer, autumn, or winter, care must be taken to water them, and in doing this not to wash the soil over the edges of the pot. As I mentioned earlier speaking of a certain locality where the Blechnum boreale grows remarkably well, cover the soil over with moss, and place the pot in a little moss basket. A skeleton of the same might be easily made with a bit of wire, and the moss inlaid.

The plants may be placed in the miniature greenhouse at once; but, if the weather be sunny, and the window fully exposed; the most simple method to give the newly-potted plants a little shade is to attach a newspaper to the roof of the greenhouse.

Now, if you have carefully done all that has been directed, from collecting the ferns and placing them in the miniature greenhouse, the plants will never know that they have mi- grated from the country lane, from the woody bank, to the habitation of man. Moreover, you must keep them in that happy state of ignorance. When they begin to droop and pine, they are saying to themselves, "Oh, I wish I could return to my happy home beside the brook, under the tall trees! I might yet be well. Or if I could but feel something akin to the dews of heaven, my captivity would never be mourned. I'd shine with the same splendor, and not be ashamed to lift my head to meet the smile of my admirers. But, alas! I have no voice but my beauty, and that is fast becoming low and mournful. My captors have eyes, yet they see not the malady. Oh, how I would shine if I could but bathe in the dewy flood. I can hear them murmur over my departed beauty, wondering how it is I do not grow. They have done everything to meet the requirements of my roots, who say to me. 'Why don't you eat the food which we send up to you ? We shall die, as well as you, if we did not keep up our appetite.' Alas! They are as blind as my captors. They do not see that my face is nearly as black as their own little rootlets."

The plant says as we say, "How fresh one feels after a good wash !" and would have us to let them partake of that health-giving operation, and remember that they have a breathing apparatus as well as ourselves. We have only to clap the hand over the mouth, and how difficult it becomes to breathe. So with the plants when their leafy surface is covered with dust, for there their breathing apparatus lies, with outlets as numerous as the pores of the human body.

Large leaved plants, such as the cyclamen, can be easily cleaned - Image: Leonid Dzhepko

Gardeners have frequently to wash their plants to keep them healthy, and window-gardeners cannot hope to have immunity, if they wish to keep theirs in good condition, from doing likewise. With some plants this is a very tedious operation. I remember, when at work at Chatsworth, under my tutor, being perched for days up among the leafy boughs of the plants in the great conservatory, applying a little tepid water with a sponge to leaf after leaf of good-sized trees. The operation should be very carefully done, as the leaves of plants are easily torn or bruised. To sponge the fronds of some ferns is a very delicate task indeed, and fitter to be performed by the hand of a woman than the great rough hand of a man. But the roughest hand can be gentle if its owner likes, and the plant receive the compliment with the same grace as if tendered by the hand of a princess.

The readiest way to sponge the fronds of a fern is to let the back of the frond lie on the palm of the left hand, and with the right apply the sponge, moderately wet, to the face of the frond. If the plant be very dirty, empty the sponge now and then for a fresh supply of water. The back of the fronds are not so easily done; but you must be patient, and be sure to look well after insects, as they generally lodge on the underside of the fronds. If you cleanse the plants in this manner now and then, and keep their roots from drought, allowing air to circulate at all times through the miniature greenhouse, and drawing down the window at night where gas is used, the ferns will be found to contend with, and conquer the difficulties of a town residence.

Mosses Suitable for Window Cultivation

Though we have a great many sorts of mosses, yet few of them are cultivated. As seen in a state of nature, our own mosses are exceedingly pretty and interesting, but, as nearly all the varieties require cool, damp situations, they are not so well adapted for the decoration of the window or the miniature greenhouse. Nevertheless, I have been induced to grow several varieties, and hope at some future time to bring them into notice.

Waiving then for the present our own varieties of mosses, in favor of one or two greenhouse varieties, the first that claims attention is named Selaginella denticulata, or toothed moss. This variety of moss when grown in the greenhouse, is sure to arrest attention, and be greatly admired for the refreshing greenness and neat habit displayed by the plant, thereby claiming to be regarded as one of our special favorites.

Selaginella denticulata - Image: Tigerente

Though this little moss is a native of milder climates it is very hardy in constitution, withstanding several degrees of frost, as well as the effect of excessive heat, and also considerable dryness of atmosphere. This, combined with easy cultivation, makes it very suitable for the decoration of the window or the miniature greenhouse. When the plant is bought at the garden center, in spring or summer, most likely it will be in a very small pot, and to make the mo3t of the plant, it should be shifted into a larger pot, or shallow pan, the latter for choice, as it gives greater scope for the arrangement of plants; thus, with the shallow pan of moss in front, with a taller plant behind it, and a taller behind that, a little bank of flowers is, as it were, constructed, which is always the neatest mode in the arrangement of plants. The -pan must be drained in the same way as a flower-pot, covering the holes nicely with one piece of crock, and several other smaller pieces round about.

In shifting the plant into the pan, the ball of soil about the roots will most likely have to be reduced, and if the plant is large enough to be divided, into two or more pieces, let it be done, then plant them at about two inches apart in the pan, and taking a handful of silver-sand (which should be used freely among the soil) shake it nicely over the top, and give the plants a gentle watering overhead. Next, place the plants in the greenhouse, and shade them for a few days by placing a piece of old newspaper on the top of two or three little sticks stuck into the soil in the pan. The plants will soon begin to grow, in their progress throwing out numerous little delicate branches clothed with little shining pointed leaves. Once the plant has fairly commenced to grow, it will very soon till the allotted space, and to hang down over the sides of the pan, becoming a dense bed of the loveliest green. The plant should receive plenty of water during summer, and in winter occasionally.

On the approach of spring, the health of the plant may begin to show tokens of decay, the dense head of green becoming yellow in the center. The best course is then to make a fresh plantation with some of the greenest portions of the old plant, and start them into growth in the same manner as previously described. Selaginella denticulata will grow without ever seeing the sun at all, but of course it must have a little light.

A typical leaf grouping of Selaginella moss - Image: Luis Fernández García.

The next variety of Selaginella claiming the attention, as contrasting favorably in habit, color, and adaptability with denticulata, is named selaginella casia, or the blue shaded moss. This variety looks extremely pretty when suspended from the roof of the greenhouse.

Being more of a trailing habit than denticulate, the blue shaded branches hang down over the sides of the pot; or, if a stake was stuck into the soil, the branches being trained to it would form a nice feathery pyramid.

The cultivation of this variety is the same as the one preceding, and will well repay the cultivator's attention. I might add, that with this variety, it is better to have the branches totally cut away from the plant before winter commences, as by doing so, the plant begins to clothe itself in new attire, and so prepares for the spring growth ol another year.

Flowering Plants for Window Gardens

In entering on this section, I must revert to the beginning of the year and call attention to the pale snowdrop, which commonly graces the countryside in the winter months. Like the hare-bell and the daffodil, the snowdrop is nearly familiar to all, requiring little description at my hands beyond the mode of culture, which would seem simple enough, seeing that it grows like the wild ferns from year to year, unattended by the care of man, requiring no shelter from the hardest frost, but a long season of rest, and that while kindred flowers may be said to be blooming, radiant in a sea of glory.

A group of snowdrops

"Blow away," the snowdrop says to them, "I shall bloom hereafter." The snowdrop cares not to feel the soft breeze of summer, nor the glorious ripening breath of autumn. Year after year they perish like soldiers on a battlefield on flood and field; and the tread of the last is heard trooping away, the dead leader is again about to rise to put on his helmet of snow. He has never yet failed his part; and if you would cultivate the snowdrop, be like nature in your treatment, and you need never question the resurrection of the little flower.

The snowdrop, or galanthus nivalis of botanists, is one of the earliest flowers of the year, and belongs to a very extensive family of plants remarkable for their beauty. Solomon in all his glory was not arrayed like one of these a lily.

Among the members of this family of lilies which may be classed along with the snowdrop as being suitable for the miniature greenhouse, and requiring nearly the same treatment, may be mentioned the daffodil, the hare-bell or wild hyacintl), and the crocus. Though the latter does not belong to the same family, yet it may be termed a sort of third cousin, and it will never grumble to fare as the lilies fare.

In the search for flowering plants, much greater difficulty is experienced than when looking for ferns, especially those varieties which are ever green, which can be found and transplanted at all seasons, short of the hardest frost. But not so with flowering plants, nearly all of which die completely down to the ground after flowering and ripening their seed. Therefore to collect such plants the season is limited.

Thus you might at autumn tide hunt, and hunt in vain, in the fields and woods, in the hope of finding the snowdrop or some other member of the lily family. No doubt, the little bulbs from which the leaves and flowers spring are there; but they have no tombstone to tell where they lie buried. Their flowers, and their long, narrow, grass-like leaves have all perished. So, until they again rise up from the dark earth, it is in vain to seek for their whereabouts.

The snowdrop begins to flower about the 25th of January and blooms away, leading forth, ere it fades, the crocus, with its golden robes, to further open up the floral year. And then the daffodil, in primrose yellow, joins another link; and when the rich dews of May bathe mead and flowers, the hare-bell clothes the woods with sheets of loveliest blue.

The snowdrop, the crocus, the daffodil, and the hare-bell, are nearly sufficient of themselves to make six months of the year gorgeous with floral beauty. The snowdrop for chasteness, and the hare-bell for display, holds all our other plants at a distance. Truly the purple gleam of the heath on the mountains in autumn is a magnificent display of sober richness, and we could do with the whirring wings of the black-cock; but the sharp crack of the breech-loader robs the scene of its purity, and dyes the heather, as it were, with a deeper stain than that which belongs to the gleam of the wild hyacinth; the associates of which are altogether of a different character.

For the whirring wings of the black game we have soft, balmy breezes, awakening bud and flower, and for the sharp crack of the breech-loader we have a gust of the sweetest melody pouring forth from bush and tree. It may be said that the gleam of the hare-bell is the gleam of life and love, and that of the heather the gleam of decay and death. And surely to all mankind the gleam of life and love must be the sweetest.

When the snowdrop and its kindred cannot readily be found, a collection of those bulbs can be purchased for a very small sum of money from any garden center store, who to meet the high demand for those fashionable spring-flowering bulbs.

Many of these are imported from Holland in huge quantities. Even hyacinth bulbs alone, beside great quantities of tulips and narcissus a plant closely related to the familiar daffodil.

Tulips and daffodils - ever-beautiful when paired - Image: Megan Beckett

The Dutch cultivators, after growing the young bulbs on for a year or two, until they get fully matured, take them up, when they are dried and cleaned, and packed off like so many boxes of onions for the supply of the seeds men.

The circumstance that those bulbs can be so treated gives them an utility which few other plants possess, unless it be through the means of the seed, and then more difficulty is experienced in rearing a seedling than in having something that will shoot up stout leaves and beautiful flowers, at a season, too, that to raise seedlings would be out of the question.

Cultivating Spring-flowering bulbs

The proper season to buy the bulbs is about the end of September. Provide for the planting of these a few moderate-sized flower-pots, seven inches across the mouth, and the same in depth. Also procure some soil, such as that directed for the ferns, and add about a third more of river-sand to it, and, together with a little rotten compost or cow manure, gathered from the pastures or your local shop, and well rubbed in amongst the soil, makes a very rich compost for the bulbs to grow in. If you're in position to gather such, then a bag of compost from your local garden store will work well too.

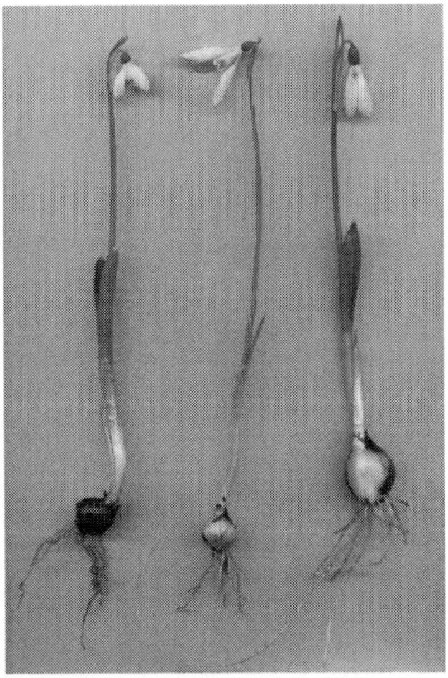

Snowdrops uprooted with their bulbs - Image: Simon Garbutt

To make a good pot of snowdrops, twelve bulbs will be required, and will cost about ten cents. Drain the flower-pot as for ferns, and fill it about half full of soil, gently pressed down; then stick in the bulbs at equal distances, and fill up the pot with soil to within half an inch of the top, covering it over with a little moss, and placing the pot in the miniature greenhouse, the operation may be said to be finished. Avoid giving them water as a rule, but from time to time examine the soil and give it as little as the occasion requires.

For a good display of crocus flowers, eight bulbs will be required for one pot, and you can have a dozen of the bulbs for the price of about ten cents also. Proceed to pot them in the same manner as pursued for the snowdrops, giving them the same after treatment which will also apply to the daffodil and the tulip, though three or four bulbs of each of these are as much as is required for one pot of each, and these will cost about thirty cents. Hyacinth bulbs cost only a small amount of money each, and are generally planted one in a pot; but, instead of burying them in the soil, they are kept much nearer the surface. The pot being drained and tilled with soil, a hole is then made for the reception of the bulb, which, after the soil is nicely level round about it, should have its apex a little above the surface of the soil.

Cover them well over with moss, and be careful not to give them much water until root action has fairly commenced, which will easily be known by the apex of the bulb swelling and gradually showing the points of the leaves. Water may then be given them more freely, and by and by you may place the pots in saucers, but do not let the water remain stagnant in the saucers, but empty them out frequently.

Continue this treatment until the bulbs have flowered; but when the flowers begin to show signs of decay, gradually withdraw the supply of water, much in the same manner as you increased it, and not do as some ungenerous people do when they have got their turn served wholly neglect those who have served them. The bulbs will repay you by blooming and flowering again if you treat them well. Also be kind to them when dressed in their full robes of beauty, by sup- porting the flower-stalk with a nice little stake, and applying the sponge now and then to keep their long, narrow leaves free from dust.

When the bulbs, after flowering, have rested for some time say until July shake them out of the pots and put them away in some dry situation, to be ready when the potting season again comes round. Where there are a few yards of land at command, the bulbs may be turned out of the pots, and allowed to ripen at leisure in the soil of the garden. And if you wish to lengthen the blooming season of those bulbs, such as the hyacinth and tulip, pot them at three or four intervals say of a month apart from some in September, and the season will be lengthened accordingly. There is another way of growing the hyacinths in glasses made for the purpose. These glasses can be bought at the seed shops.

The mode of cultivation in this way is very simple. The glasses are filled with soft water, and the bulbs are simply placed on the mouths of the glasses, the water being allowed just to touch the bottom of the bulb. The glasses are then put away, into some dark cupboard or other recess, until the bulbs have begun to grow. They are then brought forth to the light, and the water, from the beginning, is changed now and then to be perfectly sweet. The roots are also very fond of having a piece of charcoal placed in the water. Those, varieties" named in the list at the end of the book will do for either glass or pot culture, and both may be put to grow at the same time or at the same intervals, when intended for successional flowering.

Spring Flowering Plants

As a link in the succession of flowering plants to the out- going spring-flowering bulbs with the incoming summer- flowering plants, the Cineraria and Calceolaria will be found admirable for that purpose. But they are very subject to the aphid, or greenfly; and beside this drawback, the window gardener could never hope to be able to tide the plants successfully over the winter unless he possesses other appliances.

All this reduces the importance of these plants for window culture to a minimum. But those who can spare a few dollars to purchase flowering plants from the garden center in early spring, may hope, by paying attention to the following hints on the cultivation, to realize a good display of flowers for their trouble:

In proceeding to buy a few spring flowering plants, it is almost necessary for me to go along with you to the garden center. As very probably you will become captivated at the sight of some plants beautifully in flower; and ere you have had them for a week with you at home, their brilliancy will have departed, and has you disappointed. Besides, I shall be the better able to point out to you a few other plants worthy of notice.

And now we have stepped out to the sunny exterior of the garden center, where thousands of all sorts of plants are reared to meet the demands of all comers. It is May, and we are marshalled forward by some civil guide to the cinerarias. "Oh, there's a charming one!" you might say. Yes, that one has been charming for some time, and the sooner ready to fade. See, here is one just bursting the calyx, or flower-cup, disclosing the crimson-tipped petals of the corolla. Buy this one. It is much more interesting and worth of pride watch the numerous flower-buds that have yet to open, imagining that you have done it all yourself. Certainly, the buds would never open unless you did your part.

When the cineraria have got to their fresh quarters, they must never be compelled to cry out for water by the little buds hanging their heads, and the leaves becoming dirty for the want of the sponge. And if you give them a nice light situation in the miniature greenhouse, the plants will thrive, and the buds will open, repaying the attention by remaining in flower for a considerable time.

We come now to the calceolaria, with its many curious little purses for flowers. What a brilliancy they give to the plant, yes; but you must not buy one full in flower, or it may grieve you in the same way as the ciueraria. There is one with its richly-colored flowers bursting the little green calyx. That one will do capitally; buy it, and treat it just as you have done the cineraria through the flowering season, supporting the flower-stems by tying them to neat wooden stakes, not too crowded together, and the plants will grow and display it's pretty-colored purses to the best advantage. But, after all, what a deceitful thing it is to boast of purses when they are full of nothing but emptiness.

Typically a greenhouse is where stems are grafted upon roots, and leaves turned into plants, with many other curious operations connected with the propagation of plants. Let us go to the garden store, and look at the sow-breads.

Well, this will be the last at present. Their beauty is irresistible. But will they live?

The answer is yes, for years; and with little attention, the little plant will display for your amusement the loveliness of its numerous little shuttlecock-like flowers. The cyclamen likes plenty of water during the growing and flowering season. Afterward the supply may be shortened; but not so as the soil to become thoroughly dry, and the plants should be placed in the airiest part of the greenhouse through the summer months, where it will ripen off its leaves, and lose them. About August, the plants should be re-potted, not necessarily into a larger pot, but into a clean one, using plenty of sand among the soil, taking care to keep the bulbous root (called a corm in this instance) just above the soil. And as the leaves begin to spring up from the corm the supply of water should be increased.

In very frosty weather the temperature of the miniature greenhouse may be accommodated to such plants by leaving the window up of a night, after the household have retired to rest; or some artificial covering might be thrown over the little structure. And now the link is joined to the summer- flowering plants. But, for the benefit of those who may have a little garden, and a cold frame, beside the miniature greenhouse, I will take a moment to tell them a little more about the cultivation of the cineraria and the calceolaria, so that they may be able to keep and propagate these plants, and save the expense of buying them year after year from the garden center.

Let us suppose a couple of plants of each have been bought in April, either seedlings or named varieties. After the plants have done flowering, cut the flower stem from them and place them in the cold frame, which should be placed in the shadiest part of the garden; or the plants may be placed out -openly in some shady part of the garden, with the pots resting on slates to prevent worms from get- ting into them. Be careful to water the plants through the summer, and by the beginning of September the cinerarias will have several young plants or suckers growing round about the old stools.

A little sharp sandy soil must now be prepared, and a few small pots with a little depth in the bottom. Turn the cineraria out of their pots, and breaking the ball of soil nicely, endeavor to get the young plants away from the old stool with as many young roots as possible, and re-pot them, one by one, in the small pots.

The young plants must now be placed under glass, such as a frame in the garden, and receive a gentle watering overhead from the rose(that part of the spout of the watering-pot pierced with numerous little holes), and the frame shaded and closed for a day or two. The plants will soon become established in their new quarters, requiring to be watered every day, needing also plenty of air, and must be kept free from the green-fly by fumigation. By degrees the plants will be ready for larger pots; and thus you may grow cineraria for the million if you choose. On the approach of winter, the plants must be brought into the greenhouse, and kept growing and free from frost, until they have flowered. The plants may also be raised from seeds sown in May.

Calceolaria flowering beautifully in early Autumn - Image: Tubifex

For this purpose till a flower-pot with very fine soil, and sow the seed on the top, slightly covering it over with a little soil, then place a square of glass over the mouth of the pot, giving it a shady position in the garden, and attending to the soil with water. The plants will soon come up. When they are large enough to handle, pot and treat them the same way as the young plants from the old stool.

The propagation of the calceolaria is somewhat different to that of the cineraria. It is also hardier in nature, some varieties resisting several degrees of frost. By the end of September the calceolarias will have made several young shoots, suitable for cuttings, or if cuttings are not required, the plants will be all the better for having them taken off', as they will make more bushy plants for another year.

In gathering the cuttings, fill a few small pots with sharp sandy oil, ready to receive the cuttings, which should be made in the following manner: Take the shoots off below the third pair of leaves, and with a sharp knife cut away the lower pair of leaves from the shoots, also the end of the shoots, close to the joint where the leaves spring from; when this is done the cuttings will be ready for planting. With a little dibber make a hole in the center of thc soil in the pot, and place the cutting therein nearly up to the second pair of leaves, taking care to fix the cuttings nicely and firmly in the soil. When the cuttings are got in, they should be placed in the cold frame, watered and kept shaded for a few days.

The cuttings will soon strike root; they may then be planted, three in a seven-inch pot, and grown forward to flowering season. The calceolaria can also be raised from seed, sown and treated in the same manner as the cineraria.

Summer-Flowering Plants – The Geranium and the Fuchsia

The fuchsia is strictly a summer-flowering plant, and though we see them both in winter and summer decorating the windows of the cottages not with flowers but with leaves, such a mode of treatment is ill suited to their nature.

A fuchsia flower close up - Image: JJ Harrison

I can compare that sort of treatment to nothing else than the foolish task the pedestrian sets himself of walking a thousand miles in a thousand hours; and ere it is accomplished, be may be said to be neither sleeping nor waking. So with the fuchsia that is expected to grow summer and winter; the water given to it in the winter may be said to be like the pricks and pinches given to the pedestrian to keep him awake to his task. What is the individual term for when in this state?

To load his stomach with food might lose him the day, if not his life; but after a time of natural rest, vigor is partly re- stored, and the individual becomes ready again both for food and labor; and it is the same with the fuchsia after resting in due season.

The fuchsia, like the geranium, is nearly everybody's plant, and may be purchased at any time from the garden center; but April or May is the best season for doing so. When you get the plant home, examine in what state the roots are in.

This is done by sliding the right hand on the mouth of the flower-pot, and turning the pot upside down; give it a tap or two on the edge of the table. If the ball comes out easily, and the roots do not seem matted together but growing nicely, they are in a healthy condition. If the ball does not come out easily, and the roots seem to be matted, the plant is what is termed pot-bound, and would have been benefited had it been shifted into a larger pot. In either case shift the plant into a size larger pot, giving it a little richer soil than what it has been previously growing in, and see that the soil goes down round every part of the roots.

The soil is used for the bulbs, with a little turfy loam added to it, will suit both the fuchsia and geranium. Give the newly-potted plant a good watering and place it in the greenhouse, and if you wish to have a nice bushy plant, pinch the point off the leading shoot when about two feet high, doing the same by the other shoots which seem to have the lead.

This pinching causes the plant to become nicely balanced with numerous branches, forming, as it were, a little pyramid. When this has come to pass, you must cease pinching, and let the plant have its will, and be sure at this stage never to suffer the roots to become very dry for lack of water; also the plant would be greatly refreshed by being sprinkled over with water every evening.

By July the fuchsia will begin to repay you for your trouble, with a grand display of beautiful ear-drops. You must then cease to water the plants overhead, but do not neglect the roots, and the display will be kept up for a long time. As soon as the leaves begin to turn yellow and drop from the plant, the supply of water should be gradually lessened, and the plant by degrees set to rest until the following spring.

The plant should then be brought forth, and all the shoots which it made the year before considerably shortened, but still keeping a pyramidal outline; also shake a portion of the old soil from the roots and re-pot the plant with fresh soil, remembering to give it plenty of drainage, and a little water now and then, and the plant will soon start into fresh life.

The geranium is somewhat different in cultivation to the fuchsia, which loses its leaves entirely when at rest; but that period is not so observable in the geranium, which retains a portion of its leaves throughout the whole season, and requires rather more attention at the hands of the cultivator.

The geranium has of late years greatly increased in beauty, and if it does require a little more attention than the fuchsia, that attention is well repaid not only by the beautiful flowers with which they are adorned, but also by the beautiful variegated leaves which some of the varieties produce.

Geraniums in full bloom - Image: Jean-Pol Grandmont

I would advise you to buy the geranium in April or May, and pursue the same treatment in potting the plant as for the fuchsia; and if any shoot is likely to take the ascendency, nip the point off, and do not let one side of the plant be always toward the light, but turn it round now and then, and thereby endeavor to grow a nice, bushy plant.

Instead of watering the geranium overhead like the fuchsia, apply the sponge now and then to keep the leaves free from dust, and be careful not to allow water to lodge on the leaves for any length of time, as that will soon disfigure them. In winter, though the geranium is not actually at rest, yet the plant requires less water at the roots, but the leaves should always be kept free from dust.

In very hard frosty weather, the geranium, or any other tender plant which you may have in the greenhouse, should, of an evening be brought to the inside of the window, in case

Often the frost can put in a claim, and cruelly take the lives of your favourite plants. After the winter has been fairly tided over, the geranium should be re-potted, not necessarily into a larger pot, but into a clean one. If shifted into the same sized pot, the ball must be reduced, great care being taken in doing so not to break the roots.

In re-potting, have the same care as you had with the fuchsia, in seeing that the soil goes down round every portion of the ball, and remember to let the plant rise from the center of the flower-pot as perpendicular as possible. After the plant is potted, give the soil a good watering, taking care not to wash the soil over the sides of the pot. In the operation of potting, a little fore- thought should be given to that circumstance, which, if the soil fills the pot entirely, can scarcely be avoided. There- fore, let the soil be about half an inch beneath the rim of the flower -pot.

In very hot dry weather, such plants as the fuchsia and geranium, especially when they are pinched for root-room, will be greatly benefited by having the pots in which they are growing protected with some artificial covering, the same as advised for the ferns. The flower-pot of itself is not sufficient to prevent rapid evaporation; in fact, it rather aids that effect, which we would now in a measure prevent, being of a very porous nature and a great conductor of heat.

In summer, the soil the pot contains very soon becomes dry; and when we think that the roots of the plant may be lying thickly around the inside of the pot, we must conclude, when the soil is dry and the rays of the sun beating on the pot, that these roots must suffer greatly, and in fact, they very soon show it in the flaccid leaves of the plant; but cover the flower pot, or pop it into another, and the plant is able to resist a greater amount of drought.

In the former case, water would have to be given daily to the plant without any corresponding good effect; while in the latter, water two or three times a week would suffice, and the plant would thrive better.

Propagation of Fuchsias and Geraniums

If you are anxious to give a plant to a friend, I will now endeavor to show you how to raise a fuchsia or a geranium from cuttings, which is the general mode of propagating those plants. As soon as your fuchsia plant has made a young shoot of three pair of leaves and which can be cut off.

Without injury to the shape of the plant, with a sharp set of pruning shears, cut the shoot away from the plant beyond the lower pair of leaves. This young shoot is to form the future plant, and is now termed a cutting.

The next operation is to make the cutting; with a knife as sharp as a lancet cut away the lower pair of leaves as close as possible, without injury to the bark or skin of the cutting, and placing the edge of the knife across the end of the cutting close to where the leaves sprung from, press the knife through, and the cutting is made. If you are afraid of cutting your fingers in this operation, place the cutting between the fore and middle-fingers of the left hand, bringing the thumb-nail of the same hand under the end of the cutting, and with the knife in the right hand you can sever the end off to a hair's breath, without any risk of cutting yourself.

Without a moment's loss of time, after the cutting is made it should be put into the soil where it is intended to strike root. Therefore, for this purpose everything should be pre- pared previously to taking the cuttings off the plants. The soil prepared for cuttings is generally a good deal finer than that which is used for potting plants. If you have no fine sieve to pass the soil through, you must rub it well between your two hands, and casting out a!l the hard lumps, mix the soil with nearly an equal portion of silver-sand. The pots used for cuttings are generally of the smallest size; they are drained in the usual manner, and filled moderately firm with the soil, which then receives a thin coating of sand, and the whole is then well watered, and will be ready to receive the cuttings as soon as they are made.

In the operation of putting in the cuttings, a hole is made in the soil with a little pointed stick, and the cutting is inserted nearly to the first pair of leaves. Be sure that the end of the cutting is firmly embedded in the soil, and with a little more sand fill up any marks which have been made with the dibber. The cuttings should then receive a gentle watering, and if you have no glass shade to put over the cuttings to keep in the moisture, and thereby prevent the dry atmosphere from shrivelling them up, you must make a paper bag to put over them, and examine the soil now and then how it is for water; also take the paper bag off after it has been on for a few days, at first chiefly at night, and then by degrees during the day. In three weeks or so the cutting will have struck root, and be ready to be presented to your friend.

The geranium, and a host of other plants, may be propagated after this manner, if taken at the proper season. With only the convenience of the miniature greenhouse, May and June will be the best season for striking the fuchsia ; while August will suit the geraniums of both sections that is the horse-shoe leaved varieties, embracing all those kinds which are grown chiefly for the brilliant coloring of their leaves, and having trusses of white, pink or scarlet flowers; and the other section, commonly known as the show varieties, and which are chiefly cultivated for their magnificent display of particolored flowers, with which they are adorned in the early summer months. But though cuttings of both sections may be struck in August, yet the cultivation of plants in the latter is somewhat different to the former.

Say you buy a plant about the beginning of April; I would not look for any flowers from it that season, but I would en- courage it to grow by shifting the plant into a larger pot, and tying down all the branches that it made to as near the rim of the flower-pot as possible.

I would thereby lay a good foundation for the future out- line of the plant; and as is the case with the fuchsia, or other varieties of geraniums, any shoot which seemed to have too much of the lead, I would nin the point off with my finger and thumb, which would check it, and at the same time induce it to send out other shoots â€" a great secret of success in the training of such plants. From about the end of September, and all through the winter months, the plant should be kept rather dry at the roots. On the approach of spring, say the beginning or April shift the plant into a larger pot, and give it a good watering. As the plant continues to grow, try to lead a young shoot to fill up the vacancy.

By the end of May, you ought to have a nice bushy plant, requiring a moderate supply of water, and to be kept free from insects, such as the greenfly a great pest to this section of geraniums, which, if allowed to remain, will check the growth of the plant, spoiling the show of flowers.

Therefore on the first appearance of the enemy, you must commence hostilities immediately, pouring repellent among the leaves that they will quickly cease to be problematic. An alternative to the conventional route of accomplishing this is to obtain a paper or plastic bag big enough to cover the plant. Perch it over the plant fill It full of pure smoke from either wood or tobacco. The fumes will soon see the full complement of aphids on their backs.

Treat your new shoots with care - Image: Nzfauna

In training the plant you may at any time tie down, or lead any shoot into a gap, but none of the points should be pinched off for some time previous to the period of flowering. Thus, if you wish the plant to flower about the latter end of June, you must cease pinching at the beginning of May.

Two or three weeks after the plant has done flowering, all the branches which it has made during the season are considerably shortened, In a short time after receiving this cutting down, as it is termed by gardeners, the plant, if healthy, will show signs of life, by the points of its branches becoming thickly studded with green buds, which in course of time will become young shoots, to form the plant and produce flowers for another season.

Some of those little buds may have to be rubbed off; because, if they were all suffered to grow, the plant would he nothing but a mass of thin wood, which the plant, in supporting, would be sure to hurt itself in the struggle. But if these buds are all rubbed up to three or four on a branch, the plant having more food at its disposal, the young shoots accordingly become stronger, and capable of producing larger flowers, and in greater abundance. As this annual cutting down is the means of keeping the plant in a dwarf, bushy state for a great number of years, the roots also annually undergo such a treatment.

When the plant has been cut down, and the young shoots have begun to grow, the plant is turned out of the pot, and all the soil shaken from its roots The plant is then re- potted with fresh soil, but in a much smaller sized pot, in which it remains all the winter. In March or April it is again shifted into the former sized pot, and receives very liberal treatment until the blooming season is past. It is then cut down again, and so on from year to year.

You must not expect to be able to arrive at the same state of perfection in the cultivation of the fuchsia and geranium, as those who have every appliance at hand to bear upon the objects ; but, if you persevere steadfastly, I see no reason why you should not cultivate the friendship of flowers much sooner than that of boon companions, who, when your last shilling is melted in a flowing pot, will assuredly fall away from you like the leaves of the lime-tree in the earliest breath of winter. True, the flowers may fade, but they die away gradually; and when they can sustain a semblance of friendship no longer, they do not cut you completely, but linger with you until better days. That perseverance will lead you to enjoy a greater amount of pleasure than what you would receive with only the convenience of the bare window for the cultivation of the friendship of flowers.

For an extension of summer-flowering plants, I cannot do better than recommend a few more gold and silver variegated geraniums. They have become very fashionable as a class of plants, and are likely to remain so, but it is not on that account I go in for them, it is rather for their brilliant colored leaves. They, without a flower at all, are pleasing the whole year round. In early spring, and all through the summer, the tints of the leaves are beautiful. In autumn and on to the friendly season of Christmas, the tinted coloring of the leaves seem to come out more vividly than ever, impressing one with an idea that the coloring matter of the flowers must have escaped by some means into the foliage, so beautifully is it inlaid with crimson and gold. Besides, the variegated geraniums will be found very suitable companions for ferns and other graceful foliaged plants.

The varieties recommended to be grown are not of the newest stamp, for it must be remembered that this class of plants are of recent introduction, not from anywhere afar but from the hands of our own gardeners. Do not fall into the trap of paying extravagant prices for new sorts of plants and varieties with fancy titles. Often these are no better, if even as good, as the older varieties which are tried, true and with every year seeing whole lot spring into existence. Therefore, the sorts recommended, though old, yet from their good characteristics are sure to retain a prominent place in the lists of all cultivated plants.

The golden variegated varieties are named Mrs. Pollock, Lady Cullum and Lucy Grieve. The silver variegated ones, Italia Unita, Picturata, and Rainbow, with Model for a gold and bronze-leaved variety. Being of established repute, any of these varieties will well repay the attention of the cultivator.

Autumn-Flowering Plants for Window Gardening

With the autumn I come back to the lily family, and wish to introduce to your notice the Scarborough lily, or the Val- letta purpurea of botanists. I believe that I speak within bounds when I say that no plant, home or foreign, displays such a beautiful umbel of flowers for so little management as the Vallota purpurea. I am led to say so, not only from plants under my own management, but also from a plant which a friend of mine has had in his window for the last three years, in the same flower-pot, in the same soil, and with but a little drop of water now and then, it has never failed to bloom about August; beskle it has retained its beautiful, long, narrow, green leaves throughout the season.

I mention the latter circumstance, because some cultivators allow the long leaves of the plant to fall back to the ground and so become decayed, long before their proper time, and the plant thereby makes a very shabby appearance during one half of the year.

The bulbous root of the Vallota resembles a brown thick- necked onion, and the long leaves have nothing to support them but the thin scale of the bulb, which very often breaks, and so comes down their beautiful leaves.

My friend pre- vents that mishap by wrapping a piece of soft paper round the neck of the bulb, but not too tight as to interfere with the graceful hanging of the leaves. A good sized bulb of the Vallota, in a pot, may be bought at any time for about fifty cents. After procuring it, let it remain in the pot in which it had been growing, but wrap the plant round the neck with some soft material, and give the roots plenty of water during summer, withdrawing the supply in winter all but sufficient to keep the leaves from flagging, and the Vallota will do well in the miniature greenhouse.

Chrysanthemums - Image: Darren Swim

I mentioned the chrysanthemum as bringing up the last link of the floral year; but I would not lead you to think that you could cultivate it to any perfection with but the convenience of the miniature greenhouse. The chrysanthemum likes plenty of fresh air, and it suffers terribly, if its roots are pot-bound. Nevertheless, 'if you had a yard or two of land attached to your dwelling, I can put you in the way of growing that plant so as you might make the miniature greenhouse pretty with flowers from October until Christmas. Perhaps some of my readers may have a garden, as well as a miniature greenhouse; therefore, I will endeavor to instruct them how to proceed in the cultivation of the chrysanthemum.

At the end of May, buy two young plants from the garden center, say, Jardin des Plantes as a yellow, and Ion as a white variety. Take them out of the pots, and plant them into the soil of the garden, and as the plants continue to grow, you must by judicious pinching so cause the plants to throw out several shoots, which should be tied to stakes to prevent the wind from breaking them. About the middle of August fill a number of six or seven-inch flower-pots with good, rich soil, and make as many stout pegs; then loosening a branch of the chrysanthemum from the stake, carefully bend it down to the ground, and peg the point of the branch on to the soil in the flower-pot; proceed in the same manner to peg down as many branches as you require.

When the operation is completed, put a handful of soil on the top of each pot, and give them all a good watering, continuing to do so daily, if the weather be droughty. By the end of September the plants will have grown wonderfully, and established themselves in the pots. They may be then severed from the parent plant, and brought in to decorate the miniature greenhouse. Thus the two young plants bought in May, may be made to produce two dozen nice flowering plants by October.

Autumn-Flowering Plants: The Primrose

The primrose plant is a great favorite with gardeners for the decoration of conservatories in autumn and winter; and although considerable skill and attention is requisite from the time of sowing the seed in May up to rearing good plants in autumn, yet much of this can be avoided by purchasing a few flowering plants at that season from the garden center. After the primula has commenced to flower, the plant requires little attention beyond watering about twice a week during winter, and picking off the decayed flowers from the plant, also be sure to avoid letting the pot stand in a saucer containing water.

A primrose in radiant red

By these little attentions the primula will open its salver- shaped flowers one after the other the whole of autumn and the greater part of winter. The plants are very seldom kept after the flowering season. For those who have the appliance of a glass frame and a garden, plants may be raised from seed in the following manner:

Sow the seed in May on the surface of very fine soil, well mixed with silver-sand, in a flower-pot or shallow pan, and cover the seed slightly with a little of the soil. The soil should now be watered, and a square of glass placed over the mouth of the pot or pan, and put into the frame where cucumbers or other tender plants may be growing.

In a few days the plant will appear. When large enough to be taken in the fingers, shift them one by one into very small pots, having similar soil to that in which they have been growing, and replace them in the frame.

Attending to water, shading, etc., the roots of the plants will soon fill the little pots. The plants must now be shifted into larger pots say from four to seven inches across the mouths in which theey will remain and flower. In potting the plants keep their necks rather above the soil than under it; and if the plants be rather weak in the neck, and bend over to one side, support them in an upright position by slicking three little sharp-pointed stakes into the soil at right angles, and close to the neck of the plant. As the plants grow they should be inured to the air, and receive plenty of water. By August they will be ready to flower. The plants may then be taken into the miniature greenhouse, and tended onwards to their final bloom.

Cultivating Plants in Window Boxes

Let's do a recap, start to finish, of composing a perfectly sound window garden box.

Two window boxes in New York City - Image: Daniel DeLuca

With the protection of a screen or blind, fixed to the window, and drawn down over the plants in inclement weather, a greater range of plants may be cultivated in your window- boxes. With the above simple protection, the spring-flowering bulbs, such as the crocus, the tulip, the hyacinth, etc., might be grown to great perfection.

After those have flowered, the box might be replenished, by sowing or planting: a few pots of mignonette; and by May, the Tom Thumb scarlet geranium might be planted with advantage. Even in winter the boxes might be made to look comely by a covering of mosses, gathered from off old walls or other buildings in the country.

If it be thought desirable to plant the box with spring flowering bulbs, to make it look well, a little arrangement in planting is then requisite. You may plant a patch of snow drops at each end of the box, succeeded by a patch of crocuses, and one of early Due van Tholl tulips, with three or four hyacinths in the middle of the box; this will make a very agreeable arrangement of the plants, and will give greater effect than if the bulbs were planted by each other promiscuously.

Myriad flowers bursting in great success from their window boxes and planters - Image: Shaun Dunphy

The bulbs should all be planted in September or October, about three inches deep, and the surface of the soil covered over with moss or sphagnum, easily procurable at the garden center, if a mossy bank is not at hand. In about six or seven weeks after the bulbs are planted, the coming up of the plants may be looked for. Those that are peeping up through the soil should be allowed to appear through the moss, and receive occasional watering. In order to ward off wet or frosty weather, the blind should be drawn over the plants.

After the bulbs have bloomed, and the season be suitable for replanting the box with other flowers, the bulbs may be taken out and planted in the garden, or in a few pots, or a box, or any article that would hold them, and where they could be placed to ripen off at leisure.

Information having been already given on the subject of cultivating spring-flowering bulbs and other plants, repetition is unnecessary. With regard to the cultivation of annuals, such as the Virginian stock, candytuft, etc., for window boxes, the seed should be sown about a quarter of an inch under the surface of the ground; and when the plants come up, they should be thinned out a little, if they be too thick, giving them plenty of water, and they will soon repay the attention by blooming profusely.

This concluding section introduces something of a novelty for the window gardener; the notion of a companion aquarium. The sublime animations of fish pair wonderfully with the serene stillness of plants, and several veterans of window boxes often keep one near or adjacent to their floral creations. Our basis for this in our book is the usefulness of plants within water as a source of oxygen.

One of the most delightful amusements of the day is the fitting up and stocking an aquarium, or mimic fish-pond. The aquarium is a tank, wherein the flsh and water vegetables are placed the one to consume carbon and give out oxygen, and the other to consume oxygen and give out carbon, in such proportions that the water is always kept pure. In the aquarium, by an imitation of nature, you have a miniature fishpond, wherein the habits of fish and the growth of sub- aqueous vegetation are laid open to the observer, so as to afford him continual amusement.

The salt-water aquarium is a miniature sea, and the fresh- water aquarium a miniature pond. Both, to be real aquaria, must have in themselves the power of keeping vegetable productions fresh and growing, and animals alive, without the necessity of changing the water. The few cubic feet of water enclosed in the glass box must remain pure from month to month, kept so by the animal and plant life therein existing; and so soon as any appearance of decay in the plants, or of unusual mortality among the live inhabitants is observed, it may be taken as a sure sign that something is wrong in the structure or condition of the little world.

The principle upon which the aquarium, either of sea or fresh water, is founded, is the following:

A plant immersed in water will, under the influence of light, exhale oxygen gas; and this oxygen it is that all fish and marine and fresh-water animals require to sustain life. When goldfish are kept in a bowl, they would soon die if the water were not continually changed; for they exhaust the oxygen from the small supply of water in the bowl, and there is nothing to revivify the water from which they have extracted what is to them an indispensable element of life.

The introduction of plant-growth- however, alters all this; the plants give out the necessary oxygen, while some of the animals, on their part, repay the obligation by feeding on any of the vegetable matter that begins to decay, and cause turbidity in the water. Thus a balance is maintained, the vegetable and animal inhabitants- of the little glass world being equally and mutually necessary to each other's well-being. A few sea-snails, or periwinkles, for salt water, and half a dozen pond-snails for a fresh-water aquarium, are the best scavengers in the world; and the best of it is, they keep themselves, without putting their owner to any expense whatever.

The aquarium is made properly of two materials. The bot- tom and ends should be made of marble or slate, and the two sides of glass though for fresh-water aquaria all the sides may be made of glass, set in iron pillars, if the latter be enamelled. We prefer the former method. The end-pieces have grooves cut in them to receive the plate glass, which is then cemented, and made water-tight. There are simila, grooves in the bottom. The cement should be such as will not decompose and taint the water. The tank, if you are near a large city, can be bought cheaper than you can make it.

Having bought your tank, see that the cement or putty it may contain is perfectly dry. Cleanse it thoroughly by filling it with successive changes of water. It is useless introducing any specimen until the water in the tank remains perfectly free from any impurity, contracted from the vessel in which it is placed.

Where to place the aquarium is a very important point, and one which should be very carefully attended to the object being to imitate, in the artificial pool of water, as closely as possible, the position of a natural pond, or sea.

The first thing to remember is, that light is necessary for the exhalation of oxygen; but that the light must fall as it would on a real pool of water i. e., never laterally, or from the side, but always from the top. The aquarium should, therefore, be placed in a position where it may receive plenty of sunlight, tempered, however, by the shade of over-hanging plants, or by a screen during the hottest hours of the day; for should the water become thoroughly warm, a great mortality among the inhabitants is almost certain to ensue.

For this reason, many aquaria are made with a slab of slate on the side where the sunlight, if unchecked, would strike sideways through the water; when this is not done, a thick curtain of green baize, or some other impervious material, will answer the purpose. Do not place the aquarium in any place where it is likely to be moved, or shaken, in closing shutters, or similar operations; a grand point toward success is that, once fixed, it should remain entirely undisturbed.

The aquarium being cleansed and clear, the next thing is to prepare the ground or bottom of the miniature sea. Sand and pebbles, to the depth of about four inches, must first be introduced. Rockwork must now be introduced either artificial material such as is used for the bordering of gardens, or pieces of natural rock, collected on the sea-shore. A great deal of the appearance of the aquarium, when finished, will depend upon the manner in which these pieces of rock are distributed and arranged. They should form natural caves, in which the animals may conceal themselves at pleasure, and jutting promontories, one or more extending above the water.

These rocks should be firmly fixed, by propping them up with sand and pebbles, scooped away around their bases. No pains should be spared to make the arrangement of rock and water as picturesque as possible, as, once completed, it cannot be again interfered with. In some aquaria, this layer of sand and pebbles is dispensed with, and the pieces of rock are merely fastened with a little cement, or even placed loose on the slate floor of the vessel, on the ground that some of the smaller animals hide themselves among the shingle, and, dying there, infect the water; but, with care, this may be prevented.

Corallinale algae - Image: Philippe Bourjon

The period of the sea-side visit is the time to procure treasures for the aquarium. There are, indeed, several places all over large cities and the Internet where specimens of all kinds, both animal and vegetable, may be procured; but no supply thus purchased can make up for the pleasure and profit to be derived from collecting the whole stock for your aquarium yourself, and the specimens thus collected may easily be brought, safe and sound, to the finder's inland home; for this part of the task, moreover, we shall presently give a few directions.

At low water, when the sea is retiring from the foot of the cliffs, leaving a large expanse of weed-covered rock uncovered, follow the margin of the retiring waters, armed with a chisel and hammer; for you must, in collecting your specimens, avoid all that are merely lying on the rocks, and which, in nine cases out of ten, are dead. You must chip off' a little piece of the rock on which the weeds are growing that you collect, and bring them away adhering to a piece of their native rock though a very small fragment, just enough for the weeds to cling to, will be sufficient, as sea-weeds have no roots. Take care that there are no decaying weeds or animals on the bits of stone; for if they are suffered to remain, and begin to decay in your vase, they may be the rain of the whole collection.

In making your selection of sea-weeds, or algae, choose exclusively the smaller and liner kinds; the large coarse fuci are too strong for the purpose, and cover the aquarium with slime in decaying. The smaller and more delicate specimens are frequently found hidden under the shelter of the larger kinds, or nestling beneath rocky ledges. In every case re- move them gently, taking care that a portion of the rock on which they grow is detached wlth them. Endeavor to obtain specimens of as many various colors and forms as possible; for on the judicious arrangement and contrast of colors crimson, and purple and green, and olive the appearance of your aquarium will mainly depend. The pretty little purple-tinted coralline (corattina officinalis) is exceedingly well adapted for the purpose; likewise the pinnate-leaved laurencia.

The Common Sargassum is an interesting specimen found on the American shores of the Atlantic. The stems are a foot or more in length, alternately pinnated with simple branches. The plant is dark olive-colored, changing to reddish brown, upon exposure to air. The small pea-like shells growing upon its stems are air-vessels, which iloat the large stems of the plant in water.

The Buck's Horn Fugus is destitute of air-vessels, but the extremities of the fronds are inflated, forming terminal receptacles. The fronds are from a few inches to a foot and a half in length, olive-green color, with a tinge of yellow at the extremities.

The Dichotomous Dictyola grows upon rocks, as well as upon the larger algae. The fronds are from two to nine inches in height, green in color, forming a beautiful specimen when dried. There are narrow and broad fronded varieties, of the same species.

The Peacock's Tail Pavonia is a curious species, growing chiefly in rocky pools, where the water is still, and exposed at low tide. The frond is membranous and spreading, presenting various shades of brown, and yellowish or reddish olive, which, with the numerous darker and concentric lines, and a white bloom-like powder, spreading over and more or less modifying the multiplied hues, renders this one of the most beautiful and remarkable of all our marine vegetables. Several generally rise from the same base in erect or slightly spreading tufts, seldom more than two or three inches high, the divisions arising apparently not from growth, but from laceration, or separation after growth, the same concentric lines being continued in the same curve through all the segments.

The Articulated Chylocladia may be found either growing upon rocks, or attached to some larger plants. Its fronds are tubular, looking like a series of the cells of an orange, united at their extremities; the branches spring from some of these constructions, and the plant grows in tufts, from a creeping, fibrous base, and rises in height from one to six inches; they are of a tender substance, and purplish or pinky-red colored. This plant, and other varieties that are allied to it, are only of annual duration; but the minute disk, in all of them, is accompanied by fibres, which creep along the rock or stem of the supporting plant, fixing themselves here and there, and forming the rudiments of future fronds.

Delesseria sanguinea leaves - Image: Gabriele Kothe-Heinrich

The Red Rock-Leaved Delessaria is one of a beautiful genus, of which there are about a dozeu varieties. They are plants of very fragile texture, rarely found entire, unless growing in rocky pools, or drawn up in nets from deep water. The leaves of the Delessaria sanguinea are of a rich red color, and satiny texture, ar.d from three to twelve inches in length; the short-branched stem is fixed by a small red disk.

When this plant is perfect, it is scarcely equalled in brilliancy of hue by any vegetable production, the membranous part of the frond being of a vivid and glossy rose pink, the midrib and veins of deep carmine. Frequently small zoophytes are found attached to it.

The Esculent Iridea consists of a subcartilaginous cuneiform frond, attenuated below into a short stipe. Being an inhabitant of deep water, it is most commonly found near the low-water mark. The fronds are from four to eight inches long, deep blood-red or purple, changing to greenish or yellowish white upon exposure. It is sometimes eaten by fishermen, and other people on the coast, after being fried or roasted, and it is said to taste like roasted oysters. The term iridoea has reference to the iridescent hues of the growing frond in some of the species.

The Feathered Ptilota is of a red color, characterized, with some three or four varieties, by the feathered form of the frond. It is frequent on rocky coasts, grows from three inches to a span in length, and is attached by a small disk.

The younger branches are pale crimson or pink; the older, deep purplish red, passing into brown. This is a beautiful object, viewed under a microscope or good quality magnifying glass; the surface appears dotted with coral-like scales, and the fruit is contained in small involucres at the extremities of the segments.

The Blunt Ruscous-like Delessaria is a red-fronded species, growing upon rocks, and upon the larger mariuebo plants. They are remarkable for the production of small leaves from the midrib of the fronds.

The Lacerated Nitof-hyllum is another of the red group, its fronds being irregularly divided. It is very frequently met with on rocky coasts, growing from a minute discoid base, from which it is frequently broken away by the waves. The whole plant is in general very thin and delicate, of a pale pinkish red, varying to reddish brown. The lower part of

the frond is always more or less distinctly marked with parallel, inter-branching dark veins, originating at the base, and generally vanishing at the length of two or three inches, but sometimes extending even into the branches. The species is exceedingly variable in reference to the breadth and lacerations of the frond. The alga thrives well in a tank.

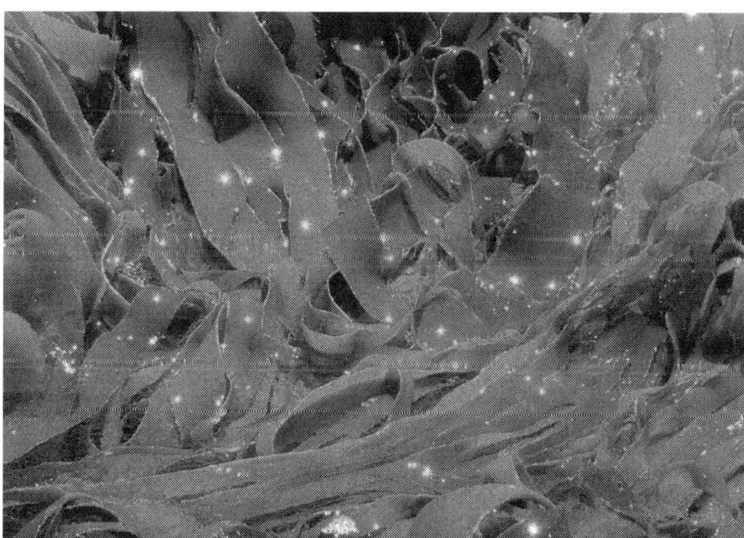

Laminaria - also known as kelp - Image: Bjørn Christian Tørrissen

The feathery bryopsis, leafy laminaria, and curly condrus also flourish well; and with the broad-leaved ulva, the purple bagnia, and purse-like cod-rain, will form a beautiful mixture of colors, that may well rejoice the heart of the aspiring projector of the aquarium.

There is much difficulty in exhibiting by small engravings the true portraits of sea-weeds, because the forms of the most interesting specimens are minute, and more particularly the details are such as can only be observed by attentive examination, aided, in some cases, by the microscope, or by magnifying-glasses. To be transported from the seaside to the collector's inland home, these specimens must be very carefully packed in damp sea-weed. The broad oar-weed is the best for the purpose, being at once stout and smooth and holding a great amount of moisture. The weeds should be replaced in their native element, in the tank, as soon as possible, before the least decay has had time to set in.

There are certain periods in each month when the tide recedes lower than usual, leaving a portion of the rocks dry that is usually covered even at low water. If possible, these times should be chosen for collecting, for a rich harvest of beautiful specimens is sure to reward the collector; and the plants that just grow below low-watermark are exactly those that thrive best in the narrow precincts of the tank. Very few of the smaller specimens will fail to flourish if, when obtained, they are quite healthy; but they must be carefully watched, and any weed that exhibits the least sign of yellowness or decay, at once removed, before it can infect the rest. Avoid brown weeds of the larger kind; they slough, and make the water turbid and offensive, and thus ruin all your efforts.

When the vegetable products of the ocean have been left undisturbed for a few days in the tank a fortnight is not at all too long and the water assumes, a clear, greenish, crystal appearance, and when minute bubbles are seen adhering to the sides of the leaves, and rising to the surface of the water, the time has come for introducing the zoological specimens to their new abode; for these minute bubbles are tilled with oxygen gas, and their presence is a sign that the water is iu a tit state to support animal life with all its requirements in the way of oxygen. Now is the time to go out on the sea- shore in search of inhabitants for the newly-organized sea; and we must give a description of some of the animals that will best thrive in the aquarium, and a few directions as to the method of finding and preserving them.

Sea Anemones

The Sea Anemone, or Actinia, in its different varieties, is one of the first objects for which the young naturalist should search if, indeed, it can be called a search, when the objects of quest lie scattered at low tide along every coast, and it is rather a matter of selecting than finding; but on this selection the appearance of the aquarium will greatly depend.

Sea anemones competing for territory - Image: Brocken Inaglory

These are the curious creatures that were once thought to form the link between the animal and vegetable kingdoms. Because they were found attached to rocks, it was contended that they derived nourishment by a system of roots; and because they put forth long and slender arms, it was contended that they had branches analogous to those of a plant ;

while, being able to move their arms, and taking and digesting food, they were held to partake also of an animal nature.

Attentive observation has shown, however, that they are not permanently fixed to rocks: they have the power of moving from one place to another, and attaching themselves anew, whenever such a removal is desirable.

When the animal is left dry by the tide, or is reposing or feeding, the tentacula are drawn in, and the common orifice closed, when covered with water, and searching for food, the tentacula are extended, and move about with a gentle undulating motion. When the anemone changes its abode, it quits hold of the rock, and reversing its position, uses the tentacula as legs. When shells, pieces of raw fish, or meat are offered to them, if not too large, they will be immediately seized and swallowed; and although the shells pf mollusks given to them may be firmly closed, they manage in some extraordinary way to consume the fish and eject the shells empty.

There are many varieties of the sea-anemone; the handsomest is the carnation-like sea-anemone, tinted in various shades of red. The scientific name for the carnation-ane- mone is A ctinia mesembryantliemum ; but Americans, who don't in general care for long Latin names, have unceremoni- ously shortened this into " mes." There are other well-known kinds of anemone, known as the "daisy," the "wheat- sheaf," and the "crass," which is an abbreviation of crassicrais.

A little below high-water mark, plenty of specimens of the "mes" anemone maybe found. The more they are ex- posed to the light and the air, the darker is their color. Thus, the beautiful pale pink varieties are to be sought for nearer to low-water mark, and in situations where overhanging weeds or stones shelter them from the sun. Those found half-way between high and low water mark are generally a fine bright red; and the anemones in exposed positions are almost brownish in the darkness of their tints.

The "crass" is generally to be sought for in crevices, behind bunches of overhanging weeds. In your wanderings along the coast, if you stop at any overhanging lump of rock, from which sea-weeds hang down, so as to form a natural screen, if you lift this screen, you will see some stones and shells which seem to be arranged on some gelatinous sub- stance. This substance is a " crass." By touching the base with your finger, you will find whether the crass is fixed on the solid rock, or on the loose sand.

If the former is the case, better leave him alone, and search for another specimen ; for he holds on so tightly, that you will scarcely succeed in detaching your crass without injuring him in such a way that he won't live in the aquarium. A good many are generally found together, so that there is no need to run the risk of carrying away an injured specimen, as a little further search will almost invariably show you plenty more crasses where you have found one. Choose two or three that have fixed themselves to small bits of stone or rock that you can cbip off, and bring them away with the stone. The smaller specimens are best, for they live longest, and look most ornamental.

Small specimens of starfish are very interesting objects for the aquarium, with their strangely colored rays and extraordinary motions. There are many varieties of this strange creature. The star-Ash has a considerable tendency to locomotion and is quite a lively object among the sedate occupants of the aquarium. The brittle star-fish is one of the handsomest specimens, displaying, in addition to its curious form, vivid hues, arranged in beautiful patterns. It is called brittle from the curious property of spontaneously dividing itself, separating into pieces with wonderful quickness and ease.

Asterias rubens, AKA the Common Starfish - Image: Pam Brophy

Touch it and it flings away an arm; hold it, and in a moment not an arm remains attached to the body. The starfish moves by means of a multitude of little suckers on the underside of each ray, which adhere to the surface over which he walks, on the principle of the leathern "suckers" with which boys raise bricks and stones, by exhausting the air between the stone and the sucker traveling, the starfish puts three of his rays out in front, while the remaining two follow behind. They are evidently affected by the presence of light, and in the aquarium will grow lively when a lighted candle is brought near them.

The Echinus, commonly called the sea hedgehog, or sea- urchin, is a great treasure for the aquarium, and may be seized as a prize whenever found. They are mostly of a conical or spherical shape, divided into five segments, covered with minute holes, from which project tentacles, serving as organs of locomotion, touch, etc. The surface of the body is covered with shelly spines, of various formsand thicknesses. The mouth is in the center; they feed upon marine productions.

Mussels are bivalve mollusks, living in strong shells of an oblong triangular form, terminating in a point. The head of the animal is situated toward the point, near the hinge. Mussels abound on rocks, and the piles of piers and quays, to which they attach themselves by bunches of strong fibres.

When they move, which they sometimes do, they thrust a tongue-like foot out of the shell, and fixing it some way in advance, draw themselves onward. The mussel should al- ways have a place in the aquarium. It is a very hardy creature, and although familiar to everyone, is by no means an uninteresting object of contemplation. It especially commands our admiration, whenever, by means of its byssus (formed by a number of silk-like threads), it anchors itself to the sides of the tank, becoming so fixed that it would take pretty considerable force to dislodge it.

Barnacles are often to be found upon the sea-shore, drifted thither upon the wood of a wrecked ship, or other floating body. We have seen a ship's mast, which had long driven about at sea, literally covered with them. They are often found clinging in great numbers to the bottoms of ships, greatly retarding their speed. They grow or live in clusters, each barnacle consisting of a membranous branch or arm, which is fixed to some body, the animal being invested with compressed shells, attached to the pedicel. The larger barnacles cluster with the smaller in the same group, and form bunches of various sizes. They are furnished with many tentacles, with which they gather their food.

When ships covered with the barnacle arrive in our ports, the barnacles are eagerly scraped off by men, who take them for sale as marine curiosities, or who make their delicate white porcelain-like shells into some kind of fancy shell-work. The barnacles themselves are eaten on some coasts of Africa, where they are very abundant. The shell of this animal is at the end of a long fleshy stalk, generally of a purplish red, sometimes of a bright orange color, and is of the form called multivalve, being composed of five pieces or valves, two of them on each side of the animal, and a narrow piece down the back. It is a pretty shell, clear and brittle, of a white color, tinged with pale blue.

The Common Crab is too well known to require a description of its peculiarities of form; but there are interesting facts connected with the history of its species which are not commonly understood. Some few species of crabs penetrate to a considerable distance inland, and are compelled to re- turn to the sea at the period of spawning. Among the marine species, the majority do not quit the shores, while others are found at great distances in the high seas, where they can rest only on the floating banks of sea-weeds, so abundant in the tropics. Some species again frequent only the rocky parts of the coast, while others prefer sandy shoals, in which they can bury themselves.

Common shore crab, 'Carcinus maenas' - Image: D. Hazerli

The most remarkable facts in connection with their history, are their periodical moulting, and the metamorphoses which they undergo in the early stages of their existence, some very curious creatures, long regarded by naturalists as a distinct genus, zoea, have been discovered to be the larvae of crabs, into which they ultimately be- come transformed.

These transformations take place when the crabs are of very diminutive size, little larger than a flea; and hence they are not open to ordinary observation, but may be seen with the aid of a microscope, or a powerful magnifying glass. At first the young crab appears with a curiously helmeted head, surrounded by numerous lengthy processes, and having large sessile eyes; in the second stage it presents more of the crab-like character, the abdominal organs being more fully developed. A similar metamorphosis takes place among both the highest classes of cetacean; and in their earlier stages of development they very nearly resemble each other, though they may differ very widely when fully developed.

Conclusion

In reading this primer, I hope that you have been spurred to imagination with your window garden. Perhaps you have even taken the plunge and are beholding the first shoots and saplings even now.

Equipped with a good knowledge of the best plants to grow within your window box, and a hardy number of tips to guard against their being damaged or destroyed, you can bestow colour splendid and natural upon your home. Where once lay only the pedestrian everyday furnishings and usual appliances of the home, there are ornaments of nature more stunning and striking than anything artificial simply bought and placed.

The examples and ideas contained within this compact book are however just the beginning. As mentioned early in the book, the types of plants which can flower and flourish brilliantly within the home are numbered in the thousands. A truly unique and novel window garden is not simply likely or probable if you continue with the hobby: it is a certainty.

21438298R00066

Printed in Great Britain
by Amazon